CONFESSIONS OF AN ANGRY MAN

CONFESSIONS OF AN ANGRY MAN

Brent Hofer

CONFESSIONS OF AN ANGRY MAN

You can write to the author at brentchofer@gmail.com.

A portion of the profits from the sale of this book will be donated to the organization that helped change my life. ARMS believes it's not enough to manage anger. Year after year, they prove that recovery is possible. I'm living proof.

As We Begin...

You've already surmised that this is not a scientific book about anger. There are many of them. Rather, this is the story of my moving from a life of anger to a new experience of rest, joy, and love. A number of transformations needed to happen in my thinking and behaviors in order to bring me to this new place. If you are angry, I hope these happen for you.

1

I have been angry almost my whole life. I'm talking about the type of anger that resembles a landmine. You don't always see it, but it is there, buried in the personality, and when something triggers it, people get seriously hurt.

Anger came early. At five years of age I was taught the piano. If I made a mistake, I would beat the fingers that failed me by hitting them with the other hand while raging at my failure. I would pound my fingers into the keys. Most of my music practices became exercises in frustration rather than music preparation. As the years continued, I would inwardly become furious with my parents. By the time I reached twelve I sensed I was on a wrong path.

One day, while rehearsing, I was frustrated over my inability to play a passage. I could feel the outrage gripping me. I sensed deep in my heart that I needed to stop this fury or it would overtake me. I knew that God had spoken to me, but the anger did not end.

Eventually, my wrath extended to my mother. I would argue and fight with her, my voice raised in volume as I lashed out at her. I became cold and distant toward her. And the anger grew. I no longer was angry only at my inabilities and mother, but now those outside my family.

At six feet four inches tall, one of the tallest athletes in the school, I longed for success. I dreamed of being a basketball star. My coach did not share my perspective and I spent most of my senior year sitting on the bench. At one point he told me, "When I teach the team something new, you are the first to mess it up." That pointed finger of failure from my coach infuriated me. My resentment toward him grew.

At that time there was a song called, "Murder in My Heart for the Judge." To get ready for games I would sing, "Murder in My Heart for the Coach." I fueled myself for games with anger.

When I didn't play, I would angrily change out of my unused uniform, no need to shower, and storm out of the locker room. It was just another failure. I hated failure and failure made me mad.

My anger didn't change in college. It just became open. I was irritated at the administration for not meeting my expectations. I wrote a hostile note to the school, blaming them for what I saw as their poor performance. I sent copies of that letter to the college president, the dean of students, and the vice president of the college.

My father began calling me "the angry young man."

At the end of my junior year, I met Sherry. She was brilliant, beautiful, and the most alive human I had ever known. When she looked at you there was fire in her eyes. I was smitten from the beginning and soon fell in love with her. She, however, did not fall in love with me. My response was to reject her outright. Pained by her rejection of my love for her, I hardened my heart against her.

We attended a small, private college. Everyone knew everyone else. I would run into her on campus, in the cafeteria, and in chapel services. I ignored her and refused to speak to her. If she was in a room, I would walk out. I would leave her in tears, unable to comprehend how a man who loved her would treat her so badly. I left college with an aching wound in my soul.

A failure at love.

After college I began to look for work.

I grew up on the West Coast of the United States and loved the mountains and the ocean. I was a scuba diver and explored the underwater wonders of the ocean, lakes, and rivers, and flew my hang glider off sand dunes and mountains. Additionally, I began to rock climb.

This was the life of adventure that I loved and lived!

Yet, the only job offered to me was in Kansas. No mountains. No ocean. Absolutely no friends. Just table top flat wheat fields.

I hated it.

Adding to that pain, my job was something I did not care for. I worked for a non-profit organization that offered important services to people. I really didn't care for the people I served. In fact, I despised the work. I was arrogant toward my boss and judgmental of some of the people we served.

What was new is that now I was mad at God. I hated that this was the best he could do for me. He put me in a miserable place, without friends, with nothing to do in my time off, working for people I didn't care for or love. (I should add, for anyone I served in Kansas, that I did come to love working for them.)

In one particularly mean moment, I wrote a note to a young woman—I had once dated her—to tell her the dictionary definition of mental depression. Later I discovered that she was seeing a counselor for emotional problems. I cannot imagine the pain I inflicted upon her.

Eventually, my boss asked me to resign, stating that this wasn't the career for me, but if I wanted to pursue it, I should go back to college to become better equipped.

I was a failure as a musician, failure as an athlete, failure in my relationship with my mother, failure in love, and now a failure in my career.

Along with anger, in my twenties and thirties I began to suffer from anxiety and fear to the point of experiencing acute anxiety attacks. I went to bed one night and awoke in the morning terrified by fears I could not comprehend. I was not afraid of something. I was just filled with the emotion of fear.

It was as if my mind was a castle in the woods. I closed all the doors and shut the windows and, as darkness fell, I went to sleep, stories high in the castle. However, during the night, all the doors and windows meant to protect me from danger, opened, and in the darkness wolves came silently into the castle. I awoke in the morning and my bed was surrounded by ravenous wolves. For the next three days, inside my thoughts, I was running for my life—terrified I would ultimately lose my sanity, and clinging to anything that might give me hope that I would not lose my mind.

It took many months to recover from that episode, and I spent the rest of my thirties, forties, and into my fifties doing everything I could to make sure I never returned to that place again. This fear of fear justified my anger whenever I couldn't control life.

And yet something wonderful happened. At forty-two years of age my phone rang. On the other end of the line was Sherry. Twenty-two years later, it was Sherry. During our three-hour conversation she declared that she had never married and knew I had never married. She told me she always liked me in college and wondered if we could start over again and see what happens.

The world turned on its axis.

A little over a year later we were married. Two years later we had Ellie and then nineteen months after that we had Nikki. Life to me should have been good. I was married to the love of my life with two precious daughters, doing work I enjoyed. But there was a problem and Sherry saw it. As she said to me, "You base all your decisions on fear, and so you have to control others so you aren't afraid. And when you cannot control them, you become angry."

Apparently, while living by myself, I had rage under control. Or so it seemed. But with a wife and two daughters, my world was turned upside down, and I found that often they annoyed me greatly. Within the first year of our marriage, the woman who had encouraged Sherry to call me and played matchmaker in our lives, gave Sherry an airline ticket to get away from me, if need be—at Sherry's request. I often would explode in fury, slamming my fist onto tables, kicking the kitchen garbage across the floor, and frequently criticizing Sherry for what I saw as her failures to live up to my expectations of a wife.

Over the years, living with me was like living through one tornado after another. I remember returning to Kansas for a wedding. A week before, 55 tornadoes hit the Midwest plains. The highest winds were 268 miles per hour with 19 people losing their lives in Kansas alone. I drove around shocked by the destruction of lives and property.

A member of my old church shared his story. As he heard the alarm sirens he looked outside and saw the tornado coming toward him. Looking for a safe place to hide he dove into his bathtub. It didn't feel protected so he quickly looked for another place to take refuge. As the tornado came closer he climbed into a closet and closed the door, praying for God to save his life.

He heard the tornado over his house as he cowered in the dark. Eventually the sound diminished and when he opened his eyes, he saw light. He looked up and saw blue sky. He opened the door of his closet. The four walls of his closet were all that was left standing in his home. The rest was destroyed.

Life with me was like living through just such a tornado. I would explode in rage. Whether frustrated with life circumstances, or irritated and angry with my family's behaviors, I would criticize and gripe at them repeatedly. After the rage had passed I would calm down, apologize, and move on as if nothing had happened.

What was really happening? My family was emotionally devastated by my angry words, cruel accusations, and unbridled rage. Everyone was walking on eggshells until the next outburst of damaging energy. And these outbursts of angry control and domination brought emotional sickness to the health and well-being of my family. Nikki became a pleaser, doing her best to keep me happy so I wouldn't explode. Ellie dug bloody holes in her skin so she could feel emotionally and Sherry felt worthless—like a non-person. This cycle of explosion, apology, and false peace occurred for almost twelve years of our marriage. I knew something was terribly wrong. I pleaded with God to change my life—to transform me into a good husband and father.

He answered that prayer. But not the way I expected.

I compare it to the time my college friend Rodger and I decided to climb Smith Rock in central Oregon. This monument at one time offered the most difficult rock climbing in the United States. Situated by the Crooked River, its rock face climbs 600 feet into the air. We saw a crack in a cliff wall approximately 200 to 300 feet high and decided to climb it. We chose climbing the crack because generally they're easier to climb and you aren't out in the open air. It felt much more secure.

Rodger, being more experienced, led the way as I held the safety rope. Every ten feet or so he would attach a piece of rock protection into the cliff and then thread his rope into it. If he was ten feet above the protection, he would fall not just the ten feet but another ten feet below the safety equipment until the rope wrapped around it and the tension and my holding it stopped him. I was quite happy he was leading the climb.

At a hundred fifty feet above the river the crack in the rock disappeared and we climbed out onto a small ledge on the open face. For the first time, I saw how high we were. As I looked down I came to the conclusion that we were in way over our heads. I thought we might lose our lives. Fortunately, we found the crack started again about ten feet away from us and into it we climbed.

At this point the crack was so deep into the cliff and the two walls were so close together that the only way to climb was by wedging our knees into the rock in front of us and our backs and behinds into the wall behind us. With few hand holds and foot holds, we were holding ourselves in place by mere friction. Added to that, it was almost pitch black in the crack. We were climbing blind.

"Brent! Pray for me," cried Rodger, somewhere up in the crack. "I'm stuck with no handholds. I don't know how long I can hold myself!"

I was below the crack on a ledge holding the safety rope. With no place to put in protection, he would have fallen all the way down the crack, onto me, and then off the ledge into space. If he hit me hard enough I might have dropped the rope and then he would have fallen a hundred fifty feet to the ground.

I prayed.

Then I heard relief in Rodger's voice. He shouted high above me in the dark that he had found a hand hold. In a while he was at the top of the cliff. He rested for a long time and then told me to climb. Halfway through the crack I had the same experience he had. There seemed to be no way to climb higher and all that was keeping me from falling was the friction between my knees and back on the rock. I had no idea what to do and so I cried out for help. In the darkness I faintly heard Rodger's voice high above me. He told me to reach as high as I could. In the dark I stretched and my hand fell into a hole in the wall, shaped like a small rung on a ladder. I pulled up and soon was at the top with him.

Our troubles were not over.

Our plan at the beginning of the climb was to walk off the top of the cliff and down a trail. That was not possible. We had mistakenly misjudged where we were at the bottom of the cliff. We weren't at the top of the cliff. We were at the top of a four-foot wide ridge with hundreds of feet to the river in front of us and hundreds of feet to the ground behind us. Our lives were still at stake. We needed to change course. But how?

In the darkness and despair of my marriage, something catastrophic happened to show me that I needed to change. I prayed for my angry behaviors to stop. But I needed to do more than stop my behaviors. My fury came from beliefs held deeply in my mind. Those beliefs supported my rage. They needed to be changed for the behaviors to stop. Trust me, it wasn't easy.

The beliefs that supported my actions were numerous.

1. Sherry is out to hurt me.
2. I have to control Sherry so she doesn't hurt me.
3. I have to change our children.
4. It is my family's job to make me happy.
5. I have a right to be angry with my family.
6. My family should be gracious to me and cut me some slack when I am angry.
7. My needs are most important.
8. I have to control life so I can be safe.
9. I have to look out for myself since no one else will.
10. I have to be in charge since I am the man.
11. My beliefs are always right and Sherry's are wrong whenever we disagree.
12. I have to win arguments.
13. I should have my way in what happens with our possessions, children, and finances.
14. It is important that Sherry understand me.
15. Keeping me comfortable is most important.
16. Sherry should not present me with any problems. She should solve them herself.
17. Sherry is attacking me.
18. I know more than Sherry and I have to keep my own counsel and ignore hers.
19. It is okay for me to touch Sherry's body whenever I want to.
20. I need to do whatever I can to avoid fear.
21. Life has to go my way for me to be happy.

To give you a picture of how pervasive anger was in my life, I estimated I had 837,841 episodes of anger, control, and domination in the thirty-nine years from age eighteen until fifty-seven. That is an average of nearly sixty incidents per day. That's sixty—not sixteen, and definitely not six.

Something had to change.

Actually, a lot had to change.

I prayed for God to change my life, and he did, but not the way I imagined. Following God's leading, Sherry, Ellie, and Nikki left me and moved two thousand miles away.

Add husband and father to my list of failures.

Now I not only was angry and fearful, but also more alone than ever.

2

Dear Sherry,

I have become aware how in our marriage I so often wounded your spirit rather than protected, blessed, and nourished your spirit. I did this primarily at the beginning of our marriage through my criticisms of the housekeeping and finances. I made you feel foolish and putdown by me. I criticized your use of time, wondering how you could run a company, when in truth I have never accomplished anything like you did when you were a manager at REM-Indiana, Inc.

I don't know how you have endured. You must love me tremendously and longed for me to be tender and kind to you. I have been so blind to how I have wounded your heart and how self-centered and selfish I have been. I have been so quick to point out what I saw as your faults and so defensive to my own faults and sins. I have insisted that you be perfect and have extended little if any grace to you, but have expected that you be gracious to me. I don't even know how to begin to make amends for my ungodly, self-centered, unloving behavior. I am sick inside to realize how I have treated you for so many years. My selfishness is sickening and has brought such pain and heartache to you, Ellie, and Nikki, and to so many others.

When you are ready to talk, I am ready to listen to your heart and not defend myself anymore, but learn and accept what you have to say. You have told God's truth to me so many times in the past and I refused to listen. I will not do that anymore. You have been and are God's gift and treasure to me, and I will not despise the precious wife you are.

Love, Brent

I sat in my car sobbing as my pastor told me over the phone that my family had left me. It was the worst moment of my life. Yet it caused me to give up the otherwise endless fight against my wife. What I saw as her false accusations against me finally rang true. I was the problem in the family, not Sherry. This was my fault—and I needed to change.

Until then, I had not seen our problems as my fault. It was Sherry's fault. I honestly believed that she was the problem in our family. If she would change her behavior then there would be peace in the home, and I wouldn't be angry and upset. I was so convinced of this that one night our pastor asked to meet with us. I was certain that he was going to "straighten her out." He would tell her how she needed to respect and honor me and do what I demanded of her.

We drove out to his home and met him and his wife at seven in the evening. Within minutes, I painfully realized this was not a meeting to straighten out Sherry. Instead, Sherry was going to let me know what I was doing wrong, and our pastor and his wife were there to support her. Of course, I was upset!

Sherry said when Ellie was six weeks old and crying, I yelled at Ellie to "Shut up!"

In front of our pastor, I shouted at Sherry: "I have never done such a thing. Only a monster would behave like that!"

For hours the session continued as I denied Sherry's accounts, unwilling to admit that I had ever done anything wrong in our marriage. Finally, after eight hours, we left at three in the morning. I was exhausted and embarrassed for being called onto the carpet.

On another occasion, my wife's sister and brother-in-law came to see if they could help us. I was defensive and unwilling to resolve anything with Sherry. Instead, I was angry at her for revealing our dirty laundry to others.

One night, after correcting my daughters, thinking I had handled the situation well, I asked Sherry for her opinion of how I had handled it. I wanted to hear her affirmation. Instead, she told me I had been harsh and angry with the girls. On hearing this I became tense, raised my voice, and denied I had done anything wrong. Then, I accused her of disciplining the girls in anger. Whenever Sherry confronted my angry behaviors, I minimized my actions and instead threw blame on her.

This behavior of denying I had done anything wrong continued year after year.

And, of course, my anger wasn't just triggered by Sherry.

Early in our marriage I chose to become angry at a co-worker whose schedule change removed him from a project of mine. I had depended on him. After the phone call, I kicked a bag of garbage across the kitchen floor, tearing it open and strewing the contents across the floor. I then stormed out of the house. I walked the streets in anger. I cursed his failure to honor his promise to me.

Upon arriving back home, Sherry told me that I needed to get help. I was hurt. I thought it was no big deal that I had chosen to become furious. Instead, I became upset over her comment that I needed professional help. *She* was overreacting. I refused to face the truth. Seeking professional help would mean admitting I had a serious problem. I hated feeling like a failure.

Sadly, I took out my anger not just on Sherry, but also on Ellie and Nikki.

Sherry would try to confront me on the seriousness of my harshness with and rage toward Ellie and Nikki. Instead of admitting I was wrong, I always became defensive. I would shift the blame onto Sherry and deny the impact I was having on my daughters. I couldn't admit how terrible I was behaving. It was too painful.

For some reason, I can't remember lots of other stories.

I suspect it has to do with *frequency.* Let me illustrate: In my life I have eaten more than 68,000 meals. However, I can remember only about twenty of those dining experiences. I can't remember most of my angry actions because I committed tens of thousands of them.

Additionally, I deliberately tried to erase them from my mind.

Refusing to take responsibility for my anger, and the pain it caused, only made my life worse. Instead of maintaining control, I lost my family, lost emotional intimacy with Sherry, and lost the ability to raise our daughters.

On top of all that, I became a financial failure.

I still needed to pay the utilities and mortgage on our home. With Sherry and the girls living with her family back East, I also needed to pay for their expenses. The financial drain was incredible.

A concerned friend asked why I didn't ask a judge to order Sherry to return our daughters. Fortunately, I had heard enough about custody battles to know that was not what I wanted. I didn't want to fight Sherry anymore. Instead, I wanted to reconcile with her. I had a legal right to see my daughters and not have them taken to another state. Since I was the one who had caused the problems, however, I needed to pay the price—no matter how painful.

Sherry's family was quite unhappy with how I had treated Sherry and our daughters. Some of them encouraged Sherry to divorce me and move on with her life.

What's more, instead of me raising my daughters, Sherry's brother-in-law was the father figure in their lives.

I needed to learn a new way to respond when confronted with my faults.

My first response was denial. Again, I would absolutely deny what I had done and blame Sherry.

My second response was admitting my faults, but then living in shame without doing anything to change. I dreamed of the day when I could leave Oregon, move somewhere else, and escape my past. Of course, the guilt over my behaviors was great. For weeks after my family left I would come home from work, throw TV dinners in the microwave, turn on the television, and watch for three to four hours. All I was doing was medicating my pain.

Finally, I decided to get rid of the TV and face my pain.

At long last, I was ready to take responsibility and do whatever needed to be done to change my thinking and behaviors.

I joined a recovery program.

For more than two years, once a week, I was in a support group where I was confronted with what I had done to my family and what I needed to do to change. That included weekly readings, difficult homework, and putting into practice what I had been taught. All of this was necessary in order for me to truly take responsibility for how I had destroyed other people's lives.

There was nothing enjoyable about it. For the longest time I fought the feeling that I was better than anyone else in the group. And that was because I had never been arrested for my angry actions. Yet I wasn't better than anyone.

This was difficult. In my previous career, I often had people come to me for counseling. I never thought that I needed counseling. In my mind, I was better than other people. I was here to help them, but I certainly didn't need anyone's help. The ability to be open to receiving help was fear-inducing. Yet it was absolutely the step I needed to take. Actually, make that *steps.*

With the loss of intimacy with Sherry, I battled pornography. So, I joined a group for sexual addicts.

I also did private counseling to deal with fears and anxieties in my life, and attended a four-day intensive workshop that forced me to face fear head-on. I cried every day in the workshop. In one session, I shared the most shameful information about myself to a small group of men. I dreaded it and yet, once I did, I felt a freedom. Secrets bring pain, but honesty brings freedom.

In addition, I participated in a class for men who had wounded their children and were learning how to parent.

When I began to fly back to visit my family, Sherry and I attended family counseling. Sherry would angrily confront me with how I had hurt her. This time, I didn't deny it. She was correct and I needed to take what she told me. None of it was comfortable.

When I was back in Oregon, Sherry had the girls call me every day to stay in touch. The pain of having to talk to my two little girls while they were thousands of miles away was horrific. They told me about their school, their friends, and the basketball games they played—all of which I missed. I cried almost every time after I spoke with them. Taking responsibility meant dealing with the pain I had caused and the pain I was feeling.

Thankfully, there were wonderful positives. In the midst of the pain, I was no longer denying responsibility but accepting it. There is an old saying, "Admitting you have a problem is the first step toward recovery." Taking responsibility meant I was on my way to changing and with it came benefits.

As you can imagine, I dreaded telling other people we knew what had happened.

I remember the first time I attended church after my family left. I was certain that every woman in the room would hate my guts. Instead, I found the situation quite different.

One friend took my face in her hands when I admitted what I had done.

On another occasion a friend asked where my family was. When I told her, she reached out her hand, touched my arm, and told me that her ex-husband had the same problem. He went to one recovery meeting and then refused to go back because he wasn't like "all those criminals." She told me how impressed she was with me. I was shocked.

My wife's nephew saw me, threw his arms around me, and told me how proud he was of me.

I explained to a contractor why I was struggling through my work and he admitted having the same problem with anger in his life. "You are preaching to the choir," he said.

Everywhere I went, I found that when I explained the wrong I had done, people didn't reject me. They encouraged me.

Some went way too far and blamed Sherry for causing the family breakup. It was a new experience to defend my wife for leaving me and to explain that it was my fault entirely.

To be true to the path of healing, I learned I needed to tell the truth. Every time.

An ancient sage wrote, "A man's pride will bring him low, but a humble spirit will obtain honor." When I admitted my wrongdoing, as hurtful as it was, I was stepping toward a transformed heart and life.

The pain of facing my problems was far less than the pain of holding onto my pride.

3

"I believe your husband is a rage-aholic." This description was from Sherry's counselor. I certainly believed so and had used those same words to describe myself. Anger was something I couldn't control. It was an addiction, a behavior I hated but could not stop. I felt helpless, a slave to anger. There was nothing I could do to stop it, no matter how bad the outcomes.

While visiting my parents in their home, I hit my head on a low portion of the ceiling. Immediately I slammed my fist against the ceiling— creating a large hole in the drywall. I had no warning I would act that way. I just reacted, and then felt guilt and embarrassment over how angry I had become.

Anger was something that impulsively exploded out of me. I wanted it to stop, but I didn't know how.

I was speeding down a road with a friend of mine. In the opposing lane a large RV motor home was turning left in front of me. I thought I had plenty of time for it to pass so I did not slow down. As it turned it was connected to a large trailer. I slammed on my brakes, skidded and, as it turned into a parking lot, I raced in behind it. I jumped out of my car and ran to the driver's window. I yelled that she had nearly killed me.

"You're not hurt," she snarled at me. "Now get out of here!"

Furious, I looked for a board to attack her RV. Unable to find one I stormed back to my car. My friend's response: "What in the world is wrong with you? Don't you know they could have shot you?"

Again, I was enraged and reacted. There was no way to stop my fury.

In recovery, I realized the truth. Anger was not an automatic behavior I could not control. It was not an addiction. Rather, it was a choice. I had a difficult time believing the truth.

When life didn't go my way, I immediately exploded in anger. It happened instantaneously—before I had a chance to stop it. How could this be a choice? There was no choice at all.

Eventually, I came to understand that choosing to become angry was a choice I had made for so many years, and so many thousands of times, that it had become habitual. It had worn a neurological pathway in my brain. It was second nature to me.

When Event A (unpleasant situation) occurs I react with Event B (an angry reaction). For me, not getting my way, feeling like a failure, even something as common as hitting my head on a low ceiling (Event A), triggered me to immediately respond with anger and rage (Event B).

What I needed to do was slow down my reaction time. That way I could generate alternatives to anger and rage and then choose a healthy way to respond. In other words, when Event A happens, I wanted to not automatically choose to respond with an Event B reaction. Instead, I wanted to choose an Event C response. I didn't yet know what that might be, but I knew I needed Event C responses built into my life.

Several illustrations helped me understand why I got angry and why it happened faster than I felt I could stop.

The first illustration was picturing a circle, a slightly larger circle around it, and then a third large circle around the other two. In the outer circle is the word "Anger." In the next circle is the word "Hurt." In the inner circle is the word "Fear."

Now, imagine you walk into a coffee shop. As you pick up your drink, the person behind you bumps you and your beverage spills onto your clothing. Your automatic response is to expect them to apologize for hitting you. Instead they push forward their face into you and accuse you of bumping them. You experience a number of feelings. You are embarrassed. You feel disrespected. You feel accused and blamed for something you didn't even do. While you may not have a name for your emotion, you are feeling hurt over how you have been treated.

A normal response is to react in one of two ways to the hurt you feel. You can leave the store as quickly as possible. This is the *flight* defense that enables you to get away from the angry person who is at least two inches taller and outweighs you by fifty pounds. In other words, running away is the best defense to avoid further hurt.

But what if you outweigh the man by fifty pounds and have two inches on him? The second defense is to *fight*. You think you can defeat this guy physically or at least verbally and put him in his place. So you stick your face in his and accuse him of bumping you plus a few other words thrown in just to show he cannot treat you the way he has.

Both of these responses involve anger. Why did you feel hurt? The answer is because below the hurt is fear. Fear of getting hit. Fear of feeling devalued. Fear of being humiliated with coffee dripping off your pants. At every turn, fear.

I discovered I was afraid of feeling inadequate. When I could not accomplish a goal, I felt stupid and powerless. I felt like a failure. When I hit my head on the ceiling, my innermost thought was, *Normal people don't hit their heads on ceilings. Only people like me do that.* I felt the pain of not feeling like others, of being less than others.

In my case, I moved from fear, through hurt, to anger extremely quickly. In fact, so quickly it seemed as if I could not stop it. I felt trapped in this lightning fast pattern of fear-hurt-anger.

What helped me find a way out was slowing down my thinking and becoming more aware of the emotional level at which I was living.

Bruce Perry, a psychiatrist, is credited with an illustration called "Acute Response to Trauma."

Imagine you are out on your front lawn one Saturday morning. The sky is beautiful, and you have nothing better to do but enjoy the day. Your neighbor from across the street walks over. You've never really met but you have waved at each other at the end of the workday. He introduces himself and in the course of the conversation mentions that you have a very pretty wife. You thank him for his kind remark.

You feel calm.

You continue to talk and then he says, "Your wife sure looks good in those jeans she wore yesterday."

You don't feel calm anymore. Now you are on alert. Something doesn't feel right with his comment. It is awkward.

You feel vigilant.

You talk some more as you now watch him more closely. Actually, you either stare at him or look off into space. It feels uncomfortable.

"You know," he says, "her rear end fills out those pants really well." He has a sick grin to his face. At this point you are worried.

You feel alarm.

It is now so uncomfortable that you excuse yourself and walk into your home, shaken by his words. A few minutes later there is a knock at your door. He is standing on the other side. "I was wondering if I could meet your wife. I would sure enjoy that."

You feel fear.

You mumble some excuse that she is busy and close the door. Then you lock it. In seconds the neighbor is pounding on your door, yelling to meet your wife.

For one moment you consider calling 911 but decide instead to put an end to this. Frustrated, fearful, and now angry, you rip the door open.

He is pointing a pistol at your chest.

Now you feel terror.

There is nothing wrong with feeling each of these emotions, especially given the circumstances.

Then again, what if you never are truly calm? What if you are always emotionally at a vigilance level, feeling anxious, fearful, and afraid of being hurt?

For years, I lived with so much fear and anxiety that I was rarely calm. I was emotionally at a vigilance level, always looking out for what might hurt me.

My wife said, "You make all your decisions based on fear. If you cannot control your circumstances, you erupt in anger." I could hear her words, but couldn't understand why that was a problem. Doesn't everyone live that way? In my thinking, life was out to get me. God wasn't really there to protect me.

"No one had my back but me" was a belief that started at a young age, and was solidified while I was in college.

Already living at a vigilant level and then adding the stress of starting college, away from home and in an unfamiliar environment, I was living quite close to a state of alarm. I painfully became aware of feeling alone and on my own.

I was infatuated with the most beautiful girl I had ever met. As a shy teenage boy, who never dated in high school, I was overwhelmed by her. We began dating. I was certain that she and I would marry in a few years.

One evening I called to ask her to be my girlfriend. Before I could ask, she told me she didn't want to date me anymore.

Already at an alarm state, this rejection threw me in to a state of panic that was more than I could bear. In that moment, the lights went out inside my mind. The pain of her rejection was more than any hurt I had ever known. I was devastated. I had no idea how I could go on in life.

From that point forward, I struggled with depression and anxiety. Each morning I dreaded facing another day without joy, happiness, or peace. I did not want to die, but I also did not want to live. God did not rescue me from this state, even though I had pleaded with him, so I came to believe he didn't care about me. I felt completely on my own to face the world.

In many respects, I remained in this place throughout the years, until the time my wife and family left me and I entered my recovery program. To change, I had to alter the way I thought about the world and myself. I needed to move from a vigilant state into a calm state. Additionally, I needed to slow down the process of choosing my responses.

Many methods slow down one's response time. One that I use is called the four by four. I breath in slowly to the count of four, hold my breath for four seconds, exhale for four seconds, wait four more seconds, and then repeat the whole process three more times. Slow breathing increases the amount of oxygen in my brain, which helps me to think more clearly. In stressful situations, it also allows me to remain in a more calm state instead of instantly choosing to explode in anger.

The leader of my recovery program told us that if we slow down our thinking, practice the program's process of dealing with hurt, and choose to remain calm, within three weeks this will create a new pathway in our brains. Instead of naturally choosing the old pathway of anger, we can choose a healthier way to deal with fear and hurt in our lives.

Navigating through fear, hurt, and anger is not easy. But it is absolutely possible. It is not simple, but it can be done. Everything written in this book describes the belief changes that needed to happen in my thinking so I could successfully practice processing fear, hurt, and anger in much healthier ways.

Not very long after I began to learn to slow down, I had a very difficult day. I am a paint contractor. On this particular day I fell off of a step ladder, twice. I went to the paint store to purchase paint. Back at the job site I realized I had forgotten to pick up a piece of equipment, so I had to turn around and go several miles back to the store to make that purchase. My employee failed to show up. Throughout the day it was one problem after another. It slowed my production and therefore my profits. But I didn't break out in rage. This was a new day for me.

This new way of behaving does not mean that I avoid pain. Rather, it means facing pain without going into anger. This was put to the test in a most difficult manner about six months after my family left me. Sherry invited me to come back and visit the family during Christmas vacation. Foolishly, I believed that she and I would reunite.

I stayed in a hotel and our daughters stayed with me. One evening Sherry came over after work so we could all go out to dinner. As she prepared to get dressed, she asked me to leave the hotel room while she changed. For some reason this took me by surprise. Even though we were separated, I felt the pain of that rejection deeply.

As I walked through the hotel parking lot, I continued to feel hurt. But instead of lashing out at Sherry, I began to practice staying calm. What she had said to me, as painful as it was, did not dictate my response. After about fifteen minutes the pain subsided and we had a nice dinner. Had I reacted in anger, the evening would have been over and the gulf between us would have deepened.

I repeatedly experienced the liberating freedom from exploding in anger, from blaming God for messing up my life, and from cursing the world, all because I slowed down my thinking. This gave me the freedom from reacting with immediately angry behaviors. Instead, I was choosing calm responses.

I changed the way I viewed my life. I was not alone.

Additionally, I was an anger addict no more.

4

I am afraid of being alone, unloved by my wife, abandoned... I see the fear behind so much of my thinking. [But] last night, in the middle of the night, this song came to me: "I am loved, I am loved, I can risk loving you. For the One who knows me best, loves me most. I am loved, I am loved. Won't you please take my hand? We are free to love each other: we are loved."
　　　　　　　—Journal entry five days after Sherry and the girls left me

As I write these words, the world is praying for the safe return of twelve soccer players and their assistant coach trapped two and half miles inside a flooded cave in Thailand. They have spent days inside a dark cavern. Isolated by underground flood waters, without food, they hoped that someone would find them. My imagination leads me to believe they wondered if they would die alone, cut off from their families. What gave them hope that they would live—that someday they would see the light of the sun, and once again be held in the arms of those they loved?

What gave me hope, in the emotional darkness of my life, was that I am loved. Despite the truth that I had driven my wife to reject me, I knew a more important truth: God loved me. And he had the ability to transform the world that I had ruined. I came to believe that God was working for my good. He didn't want me angry and dominating my wife and children. He wanted me changed and he had not given up on me. My life was not over and I was not alone in the dark. I had no idea how long it would take. Often I asked God if anything good was happening, but deep inside I sensed hope.

Again, transforming my thinking, my belief system, was not an easy change. While I mentally assented that God loved me, for a long time I did not believe it deep inside. I believed I was on my own in life and I needed to solve all my problems. When difficulties appeared, and I couldn't solve them, then I both doubted that God loved me and took out my anger on my family.

One day I was struggling to finish our tax returns. Our printer stopped working and I was unable to mail the forms. Sherry's mom and sister were visiting us. Instead of visiting with them and then asking to be excused to finish the taxes, I was agitated, rushing around the house and complaining how life had failed me. My whole thinking was that I must get this job done and the printer is ruining my efforts. I put Sherry in a position of trying to calm me as my anger controlled her through fear of the past. I believed that accomplishing my goal was more important than anyone else's feelings. This behavior made Sherry nervous and embarrassed and caused her mother and sister to feel uncomfortable and unwanted in my home. My experience of frustration with life and my anger toward it was more important to me than how I treated others. My feelings were of more value to me than anyone else's emotions.

Believing I was on my own made me incredibly self-centered. Oftentimes I would ask Sherry if she needed me. She would answer, "I don't need you. I want you."

I did not understand her. My thinking was that if she loves me, then she needs me. And if she does not need me, then she does not really love me. Therefore, in my innermost thinking, no one else cared for me and so all efforts for preservation must come from me. I believed I was alone. Yet, I needed Sherry, my children, and everyone else to care for me so I could be emotionally safe.

The picture that comes to my mind is that of a wolf caught by the leg in a trap. All he knows is the pain and the fear of being caught. He bites and snarls at anyone who tries to help for fear it would hurt even more. I was that wounded person who could not understand how to love others. I had very little energy left to care for my family as the majority of my efforts focused on me. Inevitably, I made my wife, children, and others feel unloved and unwanted.

No wonder I had driven my wife to leave me. However, in spite of how I had treated his children, I was discovering that God loved me. This unbelievable love eventually led me to experience life without needing Sherry to love me. I didn't need Sherry's love to live. I could live life, as heartbroken as I was by my separation from my family, by experiencing God's love.

One day, two friends from my teenage years, Leta and Steve, took me camping. This meant the world to me, for after Sherry and our daughters left, very few friends of ours associated with me. Obviously, most knew us as a couple and did not know how to relate to the new situation.

Steve, Leta, and I camped up on a mountain lake, went kayaking, played games, listened to music from our teenage years, and told stories. Early one morning I left for a hike in the warming sunlight. Traveling beside a mountain stream, with a soft breeze coming through the evergreen trees, I felt joy. I knew that Sherry and I often had these adventures with the girls. While I missed them terribly, I still felt joy. There was a peace inside of me. God was bringing transformation to my life. To be outside in creation, away from work and home, with dear friends, brought joy. It was the first joy I had experienced in a very long time. I realized then that I could live life, no matter what happened in the future with Sherry, because God loved me. He was blessing me with the pleasure of joy and I could endure the present pains of life.

The pains of my life were caused by lies in my mind before I finally believed that God loved me. One of my dear friends, in recovery from alcoholism, used to take me to public AA meetings. I found these helpful as the truths they told had similarities to my own recovery program. One truth they talked about was rejecting "stinking thinking." How often I believed "stinking thinking" completely contrary to reality.

One "stinking thinking" lie I believed was that life's circumstances have to go my way for me to be happy. If they didn't, then I was angry. Shortly after my family left, I read a quote about angry people. It said that the emotional belief system of a five-year-old child is that life should please them and, if it doesn't, they throw a temper tantrum. I was convicted by those words. I was emotionally acting as a five-year-old. I am an adult and yet I behave as a child. In that moment, I knew I wanted to change the way I thought and behaved. I wanted to be an emotional adult. This meant that I needed to deal with disappointments in a much more adult manner than in the past.

I remember an evening, after my family moved back, that Sherry seemed cold and distant. Nikki was upset and Ellie was being unkind to Nikki. I was owed $6,000, didn't have the money in the bank to pay my bills, and the current job I had was not going well. In other words, circumstances were not pleasant. At first, I was muttering and sighing to myself, swearing in my mind, and felt tension and anger. As I realized what was happening, I prayed for God to help my family. I remembered times in the past, while under great stress, I would take out my anger on my family. I realized that in this moment the only action I could take, and the best behavior I could do, was to bring the love of God into the situation by being pleasant and helpful. I understood that while I wasn't in control of my circumstances, I was powerful to choose to love my family. I was not going to let the disappointment of my circumstances influence me to choose to act like a five-year-old.

I helped Nikki with her homework and listened to her stories as she talked with me. I cooked dinner for my family and then cleaned the dishes and kitchen and took out the garbage. I helped plan Ellie's birthday party. I stayed calm.

The response of my family was that Nikki calmed down, Sherry and Ellie went about their business, and a quiet spirit came over the house. I chose to not be controlled by circumstances, but to respond in an adult manner regardless of circumstances.

Additionally, two contradictory lies I practiced were opposite sides of the same coin. One was the idea that I was not as good as normal people. I have anxiety, fears, anger, and character flaws. Healthy people do not have such issues. They are better people than I am.

I was asked to participate in a counseling session for a woman who had been horribly treated by her partner. She needed to talk with me because I had damaged my own partner but was now in recovery. The counselor who arranged this meeting, along with two other support people, were on the West Coast with me. The woman we were video conferencing with was on the East Coast. For over three hours she asked me questions about my behavior toward my family. At the end of the session I could tell that we were all tired.

As I sat with the three counselors, they began to discuss how people with anger issues, like me, have narcissistic tendencies. As I listened I wanted to say, "I can hear you. I am right here!" I felt unimportant and insignificant toward them. In other words, they were normal and I wasn't. I messed up my life and family. I was not a good person. As I drove away, I was tempted to elevate myself toward them and then realized I was trying to make up for feeling devalued by others. That is the first contradictory lie I believed.

The other side of the coin was that I am morally superior to other people. I don't do the wrongs they do. I am better than they are. I may have anger issues, but there are many wrong behaviors I haven't done. Therefore, I must be better in some ways.

Obviously, one of these lies cannot be true. In fact, both are untrue. I am not better than others and I am not worse than others. In reality, I am loved by God. That is my security and value.

Believing I was safe in God's love brought about a tremendous change in my thinking and behavior. Shortly after my family left, I remember praying a new prayer: *"I want to find my security in God so I am free to love… I want to find my place in Christ so I am receiving from him what only he provides, instead of trying to get it from Sherry and others."*

By recognizing that God loves me, I became free of the fear of being unloved, lonely, abandoned, unimportant, rejected, and not good enough. I was free of trying to get Sherry and the girls or others to make me feel loved, accepted, significant, valued, or good enough. I realized that knowing I was loved, significant, valued, and accepted was something that God gave me. It wasn't something I had to try to get from other people. Because I felt God's love, I could give love freely to my family and others. I already had love within me.

A destitute man was begging on the streets. One day a very wealthy man sees him, feels kindness toward him, and gives him an ATM card to his own bank account. The poor man, however, has no understanding of what an ATM card does. Even though he now has access to untold amounts of money, he still sees himself as poor and continues begging on the streets.

The wealthy man returns, finds out what's wrong, and shows the man how to use the ATM card. Now that formerly poor man no longer begs. Instead, he now runs a large philanthropic organization that shares resources with needy people. For years I lived as a poor man, begging my family for love, not believing that God's love was available to me. Once I learned to believe and accept his love, I now had an abundance of love to give to others. No longer was I begging my family to love me and make me feel safe.

Please understand. I still need love, acceptance, and value in my life. But now I look to God to meet those needs rather than trying to get other humans to meet those needs. Now, as a husband and father, I can give myself to my family rather than focusing on myself. The freedom from trying to take care of my emotional needs, and instead caring for others, is wonderful.

The picture I think of is giving blood. We can give a pint of our blood for others without any harm to ourselves. In fact, within twenty-four to forty-eight hours that volume will be replenished. Within weeks all of the red blood cells will be restored. We can give away our blood every other month for decades. By doing so we lose nothing and other people's lives are improved, even saved. Depending on God's love gave me an abundance of love to share with others. He fills me with his love so that I can share with others freely.

Knowing God loves me made one final change in my life. Because of my fear and anxiety, I would try to control Sherry so I would feel secure. This made her feel smothered and unloved. I would call her often to know where she was and when was she coming home. After a year apart, Sherry and the girls moved home. Sherry's mother needed surgery so Sherry asked me to take care of the girls while she flew out of state to be with her mom. In the past this would have raised my anxiety level.

Following the surgery Sherry called and said she needed to stay longer. Another week went by and she called again to say she needed to stay longer. During this time, I was getting the girls to school, running my business, and cooking meals. I cooked hamburger in more ways than you can imagine. Spaghetti and meatballs. Hamburger patties. Hamburger steaks. Hamburger and BBQ sauce. According to the girls, every night was hamburger.

Eventually, Sherry returned and I realized two important truths. One, I could live apart from Sherry without fear because I knew I was loved by God. I didn't need Sherry. I chose her and missed her dearly, but I didn't need her. Second, my girls do not want their mother to ever be gone that long again and they no longer care much for hamburger.

5

The largest form of slavery in the world is marriage.
Specifically, how a man treats his wife.
Conversely, the greatest venue of potential
transformation is the marriage relationship—
if a man will listen to his wife.

In college, I helped five friends put three sports cars in the foyer of our college auditorium. With floor to ceiling glass windows, it looked like a car dealership. We "borrowed" the cars from other college students during the night. We didn't realize the person whose donation paid for the auditorium was arriving that morning to see the campus. The third tow truck pulled away with the final car just as the president of the college and the benefactor drove onto the college grounds. They actually passed the tow truck on the street.

Knowing the license plates of each student, the college decided to charge the towing costs to the owners of the cars. I was furious! We "borrowed" the cars and the owners were being penalized for something that was not their fault. I was angered and decided I would confront the administration and correct this injustice by admitting that I had helped put the cars in the auditorium.

On the way to the administration building to make my case, I told one of the student body officers what I was going to do. He advised me not to do so. Ignoring him, I stormed into the building and was subsequently charged with paying for the tow costs.

Later the student body officer asked why I had confronted the school. He told me the student council thought it was one of the funniest pranks they had seen, and they were intending to pay the tow costs. What a costly mistake I made by not listening and letting anger direct my life once again.

I continued not listening to other people for many years. This was a colossal mistake, not only in my career, but most importantly, in my marriage. Believing that I was always right made it very difficult for me to listen to and learn from Sherry.

The greatest danger a woman can face is who she marries. The greatest benefit a man can do for his marriage is to listen to his wife's correction of his behaviors.

When you look into a mirror, you see only part of yourself. You cannot see behind your head. You cannot see your back. Those are only two of your many blind spots. Everyone else, however, can see what you cannot.

From reading this book you already know that I was not born perfect.

You also probably understand that the person who loves me the most is Sherry. Who else in this world wants me to mature and succeed more than Sherry? Her happiness and the success of our family are often based on my behaviors. If I am kind, loving, and provide for her, then her life is blessed. If I am angry, unable to take correction from employers, lose my job, wound our children with my words, and treat her like my slave, then she feels like life is a curse. No wonder Sherry has a vested interest in talking to me about the problems in my life. Sadly, I was unwilling to admit that I was immature and needed her correction.

My parents did the best job they could in helping me become a wise person. But growing in wisdom and maturity does not end at age eighteen. There was much I didn't learn during my growing up years and later on, as well.

My sophomore year in high school, I had a classmate named Harold. During an assigned "how to" speech, he taught us how to break into buildings. Another classmate showed us how we could avoid burglar alarms on businesses when robbing them. I taught my classmates how to make a .22 caliber gun out of a car antenna. No immaturity there!

One day Harold invited Robert and me over to his house. The place was in utter disarray. There was only a two-foot wide pathway from the front door, through the living and dining room, into the kitchen. Everything else was cluttered with boxes stacked several feet high. We walked into his bedroom. The walls were covered in Playboy centerfolds. I seriously wondered about his mother and her choices.

Harold led us down into his basement. It was dark. There was no wallboard—only two by fours. But on a wooden bench were 17 canisters of various types of gunpowder. For the average teenage boy, this was a dream come true!

"Do you want to make a bomb?"

Yes! Robert and I would love to make a bomb! (*What I am about to share with you would place a teenager into juvenile detention, but decades ago we didn't worry about homegrown terrorism.*)

Harold grabbed an empty glass jelly jar with a metal lid, and two canisters of gunpowder, and out the door we went. Having heard a few stories about homemade bombs, I thought that putting the gunpowder inside a glass jar might cause shrapnel, but I said nothing. On the edge of downtown was a railroad trestle over a large slope toward the river. At the bottom of the slope was a metal culvert jutting out of the hill. Harold placed the filled jar inside the culvert and then ran a line of gunpowder ten feet straight out of the hole. He then stood right in front of it.

The picture I see is someone looking directly into the mouth of a cannon and asking them to fire the massive gun. Harold bent over and lit the fuse. The roar of the explosion is not something I remember. What I do remember clearly was the ball of fire that erupted out of the mouth of the culvert.

If you are old enough to remember classic television cartoons, two characters were called Wile E. Coyote and Road Runner. The coyote was always trying to kill the road runner—usually with bombs. The road runner always got away and the coyote always took the explosion. After the smoke cleared, the coyote would stand there burnt to a crisp, black and smoldering.

That was Harold.

His face was burnt black. Robert was a bit away and lost only eyebrows and some of the hair on his head.

Harold was somewhat stunned. "I thought I used a slower-burning gunpowder for the fuse," he said.

I looked up and saw the cloud of smoke was now the size of a house hanging above the railroad trestle leading into town. I was certain that someone downtown would come to investigate, so we needed to get out of there fast.

We hustled Harold through back streets. Seeing the burns on his face, we felt it was time to take him to a doctor. He didn't agree. Once we got him home, he put Vaseline on his face—effectively sealing in the burn. He didn't come to school for many days.

The point of this story is that when you are a teenager, you often make very immature decisions. But what if you are still acting in an immature manner decades later as an adult—still refusing to listen to anyone?

In my very first job after college, my boss gave me a book to read that described his work philosophy. I worked five years for him. I never read it. I refused to trust anyone over thirty years of age. I rejected showing any respect to the former leader of the company, even though he strongly influenced the current boss. No wonder I lost my job.

After getting married, I assumed that my opinions, beliefs, and ideas were more valuable than Sherry's. As Sherry used to say, "The only way to be accepted into your family is to believe like you." I did everything I could to manipulate her into thinking like me. I gave little consideration to her opinion or ideas. If she disagreed with me, then she was wrong.

One night we visited a hardware store to purchase bathroom tile. In the middle of the store we almost got into a shouting match because I was so insistent on using the tile I wanted. I refused to consider her opinion. She eventually gave up the fight and let me do what I wanted.

Eventually, she called out my wrong behaviors. I was deeply offended one day over her comments to me. I withdrew for three days, ignoring her and her visiting mother and doing almost nothing for Sherry's birthday. I didn't help the girls get her gifts and I gave her nothing. Not even a card. Nikki was so hurt she went upstairs, found a hairbrush, wrapped it, and gave it to her mom as a birthday present.

My whole goal was to punish Sherry for criticizing my angry behaviors. I wanted her to feel guilty for how she spoke to me. I wanted her to know how much she hurt me. I believed that I had a right to pity myself and to ignore my wife's observations of my behavior.

In refusing to humble myself enough to hear (let alone heed) Sherry's words, I deeply wounded my wife. I made her feel unimportant to me. I did not see her as an ally to help me grow. All I felt was offense at being corrected.

Within less than a year, Sherry and the girls left and I spent both her and Nikki's birthdays alone.

Changing my thinking from seeing Sherry as my enemy, and instead seeing her as a partner, took trust. As I trusted God with my life, I was able to trust Sherry—even when it was painful to hear her words. I stopped fearing that Sherry was trying to harm me. When I saw that correction by her was not meant to hurt me, but was meant to bring about good, I was able to slow down the process of becoming defensive. I ceased thinking that the only person I could trust was me. I began to see Sherry as the person who saw my blind spots and who could help me succeed in life.

One of the first changes after I started listening to Sherry was the dramatic improvement in my business. For the next several years, my business increased its profits two hundred percent each year. If only I had started listening to her sooner! In addition, I stopped thinking of our home as the place where I get what I want. Initially I did not like Sherry's remodeling ideas, but I agreed to them. When they were completed, however, I loved them!

I began to consider that God could speak through Sherry to me. In fact, he probably speaks through her more than anyone else to me. This is not always easy. Sometimes she corrects my wrong behaviors and she is angry. It takes a lot of humility to be rebuked by my wife, but the result is good.

On one occasion Sherry opened up to me about hurt I had done to her unknowingly. My initial reaction was fear and anxiety, defending myself ("I never meant that!"), and then shutting down and being quiet. I felt accused. I had an awareness of shame for the hurt I had caused her, and I wanted to protect myself from further pain.

Fortunately, I had learned enough from my recovery program that I began to feel compassion for her. She needs to get this pain out. This is actually a good thing. Think of her feelings ahead of your feelings and how terrible you feel about yourself. I trusted that God wanted to heal our relationship. I needed to accept what she had to say to me. I was able to do this because I knew that God loved me.

I listened to Sherry's words. I told her how sorry I was. My response was to help her heal from the pain I had caused. Eventually, she apologized to me for becoming so angry. I told her she owed me no apology. Both Ellie and Nikki heard what Sherry said to me. I explained it was important that their mom get her pain out instead of holding it in like an infection.

A while back, Sherry was deeply wounded by someone. I listened to her instead of playing on my phone or abruptly telling her what she needed to do to fix the problem. That evening, twice she told me how grateful she was that I had listened to her. Trust me, a grateful wife is so much better than a hurt and therefore angry wife.

I now listen to others besides Sherry. Recently, I sensed distance between Nikki and me. I asked her what I had done. Immediately she told me! She told me that when I get anxious, I repeat myself in frustration, and it makes her and everyone else in the family feel anxious. I listened to her correction and told her that I needed to change. Because I listened to her, and did not defend myself, she admitted that she does the same behavior—a confession that was out of character for her. I sensed an increase in closeness with her through that honesty.

About a week later she and I were rock climbing. I set up the anchors at the top of the cliff in the hot sun. I mishandled the rope and it tangled into multiple loops and knots. For fifteen or twenty minutes she and I sat in the sun and unwrapped the rope. I heard myself say, "I don't understand why it tangled up. I had it wrapped correctly."

I spoke these words several times and realized what I was doing. It was very hard to stop the frustration I felt and to cease from repeating my words, but soon I sensed the tension retreat and we untangled the rope. We had a wonderful climb and I believe that controlling my behavior—in accordance with Nikki's correction—was the real exclamation point of that weekend.

I don't just listen to my family. I listen to others. This past summer we had a job go very wrong on us. The owner was so upset that he wanted to collect money from my insurance company. A friend of mine who owns his own painting company heard about it and called to find out what had happened. As I explained the situation, he told me that I had done the job incorrectly. This was not easy to hear. It was actually very hard to hear his words. I struggled while listening to his correction. But when he finished telling me what I had done wrong, I thanked him and decided that I needed to do what he said.

I have discovered that listening to others, especially your wife, will bring you success in marriage, work, and relationships. Listening and hearing what my wife says has only blessed my life and, by doing so, has blessed her life, too.

When I first was married, I thought marriage was designed to make me happy. I never realized it was designed to develop me into a person who my wife and others love being around. Sherry is not my enemy when she corrects me. She is, as one counselor said, attempting to produce good results.

Sherry is the greatest venue for positive transformation of my life. Always. If I will listen.

6

Imagine your first day at work. Your supervisor moves within inches of your face, screaming!

"You are nothing! You are a squirrel! I will make you into what I want you to be!" he shouts in your face.

You shrink back in shock and involuntarily start to speak.

"Shut your mouth up!" he screams at you. "You will not speak unless I tell you to!"

Imagine he humiliates you in front of others by calling you names and threatening you. He controls every decision you normally would make as an adult. He tells you when you can go to bed and when you are to wake up. He takes away your vehicle so you cannot leave. He gives you commands that are impossible to fulfill such as demanding you travel to a location, on foot, over a mile away, in four minutes. Impossible, but when you fail, he makes you work harder. He takes your mobile phone away from you. He cuts you off from your family and does not allow you to contact them or have anything to do with them. He tells you what to wear and how to behave every moment of the day. And, if you don't, he angrily increases your suffering.

You are shouted at to treat him with the utmost respect and honor. You are never to talk back to him or you will be punished. He is always right and you, merely by being you, are always in the wrong. His job is to make sure that you are broken and that whatever he wants you to do, you will do with everything you have within you. His goal is to make you into the person he wants you to be. Your identity and freedom are eliminated. If you try to express your opinion, you will be punished.

By now you may have realized that I am talking about Army boot camp and the drill sergeant.

Now, let's consider what would happen if I treated my family like a drill sergeant.

Like a drill sergeant, I expect my wife to respect me, even if I don't respect her. If we disagree, then my opinion is correct, she is wrong, and my job is to break her will until she believes the way I believe.

When Sherry and I were first married, I discovered that my wife enjoys sleeping in and sometimes was late to meetings. I rose early and often arrived five to fifteen minutes before an appointment. I disrespected her and wanted to change her behavior. I saw her as lazy and undisciplined. I put her down with my critical comments, once asking her how she could ever supervise 132 employees at her former company. I accused and blamed her for her behavior, wanting her to act like me because my beliefs were correct and hers were wrong. My angry words made her feel accused, unimportant, devalued, and unloved by me. I wrongly believed that for us to have an intimate marriage, she had to think and act as I did. When she didn't, I was angry.

Imagine that every plan for the family needed to be agreed to by me. That means that if my wife wants to visit her family for our vacation, but I would rather take our family to Disneyland, then my wife is wrong and I am right.

I sometimes put my family in danger because I thought my ideas were the best. I built a go-cart for our two daughters. It was similar to the wooden one I had as a child with axles made out of two by fours with wheels nailed onto the ends. The front board is attached to the portion of the cart you sit on, and you steer by pushing with your feet and by pulling with a rope attached to each end of the two by four. There are no brakes.

My daughters loved it as they gently rolled down a small rise near our home. One day I thought it would be a wonderful idea if we took the cart to a soapbox derby track. The track was higher and longer than our hill at home. Yet, my ideas were always good, so Nikki raced off. Quickly I realized that, since the track was so much steeper than our street, she was hitting speeds much higher than previously. Unable to steer with her feet at such a high rate of acceleration, she nosed into a giant pile of bark dust, which saved her from crashing onto the asphalt.

My oldest daughter, Ellie, didn't want to take a turn. I angrily demanded that she ride down the track. I had built the go-cart for her and I wanted her to ride it. This was my idea of fun for me and they had better do what I wanted.

Fearful, in tears, she got into the go-cart. Within moments she was racing at such a high speed that she could not steer. Again, there were no brakes. She over-steered to the right, the machine rolled over, and she was thrown across the asphalt. She cried out in pain as her bare legs tore into the hot track. Bloodied, she refused to try again.

A normal person would have assisted Ellie, expressed compassion, and apologized for putting her in such a dangerous position. Instead, I was angry that she failed to steer correctly. Furthermore, I was frustrated that she had refused to help me have a good time. In my opinion, my ideas were the best and must be followed.

I expected Sherry to put me first in her life, particularly when it came to time spent together. Therefore, there was little if no time for her family or friends. I remember thinking that if she spends time with others, then I will feel ignored or abandoned to myself. I would often dread when she flew back East to visit her family because I would suffer anxiety from being alone. Then again, I would complain to Sherry why she had so many friends come and stay at our house. In so doing, I made Sherry feel guilty and uncomfortable with her friends and family. My belief was that my emotional needs were more important that Sherry's needs. She is my wife and she is here to serve me!

The problem of Sherry spending time with others became so great that I questioned if she was having an affair with one of her girlfriends. In my mind, I am her husband and I am most important. She should find her emotional fulfillment in being with me and me alone. She has no need to be with others. My needs are most important. In my home, I was closer to an Army drill sergeant than a loving husband and father.

What I did not realize was that young men and women know, to some degree, what they will face in boot camp. They know they will be taught to follow orders and do whatever they are told to do. They willing submit to being controlled and directed by others. They know that boot camp is hard and that it will transform them into what the military desires. They expect this behavior and agree to it before they ever join the military, and they know it is for a limited period of time.

My wife and eventually our daughters expected to be loved. They expected that I would be kind and gentle. They hoped to be treated with respect, honor, and love. That is what I promised to my wife when we stood in a church and made our vows to each other.

I lied to her. I lied to my daughters.

They didn't sign up to be treated like soldiers that I commanded. They expected to be cherished by a loving and respectful husband and father. I treated them the exact opposite.

The idea of male leadership, particularly in my mind, is best explained by a TV commercial called "Mistaken Body Wash." The advertisement opens with a man taking a shower and washing himself with what he believes to be liquid soap. His wife notices and casually mentions that the product is used as a cleanser for a woman's private area. Her husband is horrified!

Immediately the camera rapidly finds him pulling a car with his teeth, drinking a raw egg, hitting a punching bag, breaking boards with his bare hand, making a metal knight's helmet to wear while mowing the lawn, and crushing a metal pop can with his bare hands. He does all of this to somehow prove his masculinity.

What I noticed is that every example reveals the man overpowering something. The ability to overpower, and therefore, control, somehow "proves" masculinity. This definition of masculinity, especially for an angry man, is extremely dangerous. If my goal in marriage and family is to overpower, to control, to dominate, then my wife and children are severely damaged in the process. There is no equality of value in the relationship. I am your master! This view of my family hurt my wife more deeply than words could ever express.

One evening I was irritated and angry with Sherry because she failed to understand what I was talking about. In fact, this was an ongoing frustration because I wanted to control our conversations. That evening, Sherry and I verbally fought and she said to me, "Your anger is destroying me." I was blind and could not see how my behaviors were hurting her. I knew I was irritated with her, but I didn't feel it was a problem. Being irritated was just a part of my behavior, especially if I didn't get my way when communicating.

Circumstances were not any better for my children. My goal was to force them, particularly by my words and anger, into the behaviors I wanted. One night, furious with how our daughters had left their bedroom in a mess, I stormed in. For twenty minutes I yelled in fury at them.

"You make me live like an animal," I shouted at them, my face red in rage. I was six feet four inches tall. I towered over them as they cowered on their beds in fear. My ten-year-old daughter tried to explain that she was not an animal. I shouted her out.

"You will not make me live like this!" I spat out at them. Spittle was drooling from my mouth as I berated them. One of my daughters was crying as I shook my finger at them and told them what punishments awaited if they did not change.

After my family left me, I cried out to God. I didn't understand why I had behaved in these ways. I still hadn't yet seen what I had done to Sherry, but I knew with certainty that I had hurt our daughters.

For several months there was no answer.

Then one day the truth came to me: "When you were yelling in anger at your daughters, you weren't thinking about how you were making them feel. You were only thinking about how you felt."

In that moment of revelation, I realized how selfish and self-centered I was. The horror of being consumed with my own interests was devastating. What a shock to realize that I loved myself more than my own daughters!

I was sick of myself. Devastated by tears, I left work and jumped in my car. As I drove home, I left the freeway on an eighty-foot tall exit ramp. Sick of my life I spun the steering wheel to launch off the ramp into the air. As the car jerked toward the guard rail I came to my senses and jerked the wheel back. The pain of realizing how horrible I am fortunately did not end in suicide, but rather drove me to find a better way to live with others.

I wondered what the opposite was of being angry, controlling, and dominant. I found a solution that readers with no religious background may or may not find helpful. However, this was the path I took to transformation.

Of all the leaders throughout history, the life of Jesus reveals an unusual view of leadership. At one point he was asked by the mother of two of his followers about being promoted to places of honor in his kingdom. His other followers were upset over this request, wanting to secure places of honor for themselves. He responded,

> *You know that the rulers of the Gentiles lord it over them and their great men exercise authority over them. It is not so among you, but whoever wishes to become great among you shall be your servant, and whoever wishes to be first among you shall be your slave, just as the Son of Man did not come to be served, but to serve, and to give his life a ransom for many.* (Jesus often referred to himself as "the Son of Man.")

This was hard for me to understand. *How can you be a leader if you are giving into others?* I wondered. *Wouldn't they just run all over you like a doormat?*

On the night Jesus was betrayed to death by one of his own followers, he did not try to stop the man, even though he knew what he was going to do. Instead, he told his disciples that they all would turn away from him and flee when the soldiers came to arrest him (something they all did). After telling them this, he then performed what only a servant would do for a master and his guests. Since they had been walking the dusty Jerusalem streets in sandals, he washed their feet.

When he was done, Jesus said this,

> *Do you know what I have done to you? You call me Teacher and Lord; and you are right, for so I am. If I then, the Lord and the Teacher, washed your feet, you also ought to wash one another's feet. For I gave you an example that you also should do as I did to you.*

That very next day, Jesus allowed himself to be put to death for the forgiveness of their sins. This type of leadership, when one gives his life for those who fail to follow, caught me off guard. I had always thought of leadership as telling others what to do. Commanding them. Expecting them to follow my orders and respect me. Jesus' followers did none of this. They fled for their lives and left him alone to die at the hands of those who were insanely jealous of his popularity and teachings. Still he died for them, knowing they had failed him.

This example of leadership was radically different from what I saw in culture. He wasn't trying to overpower them, control them, or dominate them. He had a goal, but he wasn't going to achieve it by destroying others. What is most impressive to me is that after his death (and resurrection), every one of those eleven disciples gave their lives in his cause.

I saw a very simple example of this one day while waiting in line at the post office. Only two employees were working at the counter (neither seemed happy to help us) with a long line of people waiting to be helped. A woman behind me began to complain about the long wait.

"Why don't they get more people working in here? I have so much to do today," she said. She began to loudly curse and berate the post office. My first thought was, *We all have to endure wasting our time waiting. Your complaints just make it more miserable. Why don't you shut your mouth or just get the hell out of here!* I suspect many others in the line were equally annoyed by her.

Fortunately, I did not voice the first thought in my brain. Instead I turned and said to her, "I don't have a very busy day. Would you like to cut in front of me? It would speed up your time a bit."

Surprised, she said, "Oh no! I couldn't do that, but it is so nice of you to offer. That is very kind of you." At this point the anger was gone from her voice and she was quite positive. A moment went by and then in a much louder voice that others in line could hear, she added, "What an awesome man you are! It is wonderful to have people like you around."

At this point I now wanted her to shut up again because I was embarrassed. I continued in line and at the counter learned I had to fill out a form. I stepped aside and the lady proceeded with her mailings. As she left she said to me, "Have a wonderful day. It was so nice to meet you!"

Ten minutes earlier she came into the post office cursing at the delay and now she was leaving happy and encouraging. All I did was resist commanding her to shut up, and instead offered to be a servant, and it changed the whole atmosphere in her and around her.

That is influence! And that is the leadership style that Jesus lived and taught. He moved people by his love and sacrifice for them rather than by commanding and angrily demanding of them. This was not the example I had lived in front of my family.

I finally realized that if you become a servant to others, you are set free from being a slave to yourself, and a slave to the horrible bondage of self-centeredness and selfishness. Encouraged, I began to try to put this new way of thinking into practice.

As I've mentioned before, I own a house painting company. One of my new employees was working very slowly. I became angry at his performance because of my fear of losing money. I felt powerless. I stopped, prayed, and asked God to help me not become (outwardly) angry toward him. I realized this was his first job and he didn't know how to work at the level that I desired and expected.

After waiting to be calm, I called the new employee over and *asked* if I could show him how I wanted him to work. I demonstrated the speed at which I needed him to perform his job. The result was that he went back to work at a faster speed and was in a good mood. I felt a sense of accomplishment that I was able to influence him with patience and compassion rather than by angry control.

One of the moments when I first applied this new type of leadership, by service rather than anger toward my children, was the first time I saw them during our separation. At the request of my daughter's counselor, I was invited to fly out to Indiana for Christmas. One evening, our family went to an arcade where Ellie and Nikki won some small toys. Leaving the arcade, Ellie's toy slinky broke inside the car. She became upset and began to cry. My previous behavior would be to rage and command her to quit throwing a fit. I felt tense and powerless to stop the situation. Then I thought, *What can I do to help her process her pain?*

I remembered a book a counselor had given me about helping children when they are upset. Imagining how Ellie might be feeling, rather than how I was feeling, I asked if she was disappointed to have a toy that broke almost immediately. Her crying told me she agreed with me. I then said I wished I could buy her a slinky big enough that she could climb inside of it and roll down a hill. Her crying stopped and she began to laugh! Tears turned to laughter at the image of riding inside a slinky down a hill. All I did was think about her feelings, validate them, and then express my willingness to do something that I had no power to do but wish I could.

That is leadership by influence and it showed me that, even when I feel powerless, I actually have great power to influence others in a healthy manner and change the atmosphere for good.

However, I still had a problem with the idea of male leadership— meaning serving others rather than being served. The problem came from my misunderstanding of a particular passage in the Bible.

The passage says, "Wives, be subject to your own husbands...for the husband is the head of the wife." I must say that this statement has put untold women under bondage to their husbands, and has encouraged men to treat their wives like slaves under their control. According to my old interpretation of this passage, God wanted me to dominate my wife, for that is the position of authority he has given to me. Because I am male, I am in charge, and if my family doesn't like it, then they are wrong and I am right.

However, let us consider the idea of a man leading his family the way Jesus led his disciples. If you are a leader following Jesus' example, then you must surrender your wants and wishes and instead do what is best for those you lead. You must serve them. According to Jesus, you will lead by the influence of loving service rather than angrily commanding your way.

After about a year my wife and daughters returned home and I moved out. However, my wife wanted me to have a relationship with our daughters, and would have me over for dinner. Now, I had been painting all day long and was exhausted. But at the end of the day, when our girls had gone to bed and Sherry was heading that way, I would look at the sink filled with dishes and knew I needed to serve.

So, when the house was quiet, I would stay late and clean the kitchen. This sort of behavior was quite new as I would rather leave for my house after the girls had gone to bed. I finally had come to realize that whether Sherry and I ever reunited, I needed to behave as a loving leader of our broken home.

Prior to our separation, Sherry had begun to spend a considerable amount of time with a young woman. My response was to feel rejected, unimportant, and separated from Sherry. I would tell myself that, "Sherry doesn't love me." I angrily accused her and criticized her friend. I believed that, as her husband, I was most important.

What I failed to understand was that my wife needed more social time with others than I did. I could not see that I was crushing her emotionally. She was lonely for friendship and I expected her to find all her fulfillment in time with me alone.

Later, I came to realize that Sherry needed more than just me and that was okay. It didn't mean she didn't love me. While I miss my wife when she is gone, I do not have the old fears of rejection and am happy for her to have time with friends and family.

After I realized what it truly means to be a leader, I saw that my goal was to please my wife and children. I would get up every morning and ask the question, "What do my wife and children need today?" and then follow through on any ideas that came to me. This set me free to bless my children.

Rather than criticize and condemn them for behaviors that I disliked, I looked for ways to help them out.

Previously I would respond in anger to my daughters' emotional outbursts. My reason was I had emotional outbursts and felt not normal or healthy like relaxed people. I hated this behavior. So, when Ellie or Nikki were upset, I immediately attacked them verbally, feeling I must stop them so they did not act like me.

When I saw that my goal was to serve, I began to remain calm and see what I could do to help.

Recently, Ellie was on call to work, yet had plans to be with friends of hers for the evening. Her phone ran and her boss told her to come to work. She was angry and stormed off to work.

While I don't like drama, instead of thinking how uncomfortable I felt, I began thinking how disappointing this must be for her. After she left for work, I drove to a coffee shop and purchased one of her favorite drinks. She saw me come in and I held up the coffee for her. She walked over, took the coffee, and then in front of all her co-workers and customers, threw her arms around me and held me close for a long time. (Yes, I can die and go to heaven now!)

On another occasion Ellie, Nikki, and I were having lunch in a restaurant. Ellie accidently knocked her salad onto the floor. The look on her face revealed her innermost thoughts. I could see the fear and worry in her eyes. Instead, I thought for a moment how I would feel in her place, and then calmly explained that it was no problem and everyone spills food. She began to relax. We bought another salad and continued the meal without a problem. I'm sure she wondered what in the world happened to her dad.

That same day, Nikki had been given a very expensive camera from my parents as a Christmas present. While visiting a children's museum, Nikki left it by a display. As we prepared to leave, she realized she had lost it. While not happy that she had lost a camera worth hundreds of dollars, I knew I needed to help her rather than make her feel guilty. We returned to the room where she had last remembered using the camera. Nothing.

We talked to a security guard. She hadn't seen it either.

Still trying to remain hopeful, we went to the lost and found department. There was the camera!

At the end of the day, what was most impressive to me was not finding the lost camera or replacing a spilled salad. It was that I thought more of my daughters' feelings than my own. That was the real miracle.

This new understanding of leadership—in which I was a servant to my family, and their needs and desires were more important than what I wanted—wasn't easy. Instead, it seemed to run counter to my own health and well-being (in other words, "What is going to happen to me?"). Additionally, church teaching led me to believe that men were superior and in authority over their wives.

I clearly remember as a teenager attending a Bible conference where we were presented with a drawing revealing what the teacher thought were the authority roles in the home. The speaker drew a picture of God at the top of the page. His two hands showed him holding a hammer and a chisel. Underneath the chisel was a rough-cut diamond. The diamond was a child being directed and corrected by the parents. The chisel was the mother above the diamond (child) and *above* the chisel (mother) was the husband as the hammer. That image gave me the view that men are above (superior to) women. Deep inside I saw myself having a God-given right to dominate my wife. I sincerely believed that is how God made me and Sherry.

After Sherry moved away, I gained a much healthier image of our family. It started in discomfort by a friend telling me that he had a terrible image of my family. In his mind, he saw a large and lengthy spear. Pierced through the chest were Sherry, Ellie, and Nikki. I was holding the end of the spear.

"This is what you have done to your family," he told me.

As I pondered the horror of that image, another picture came to me of what I wanted our family to become. I saw my family standing side by side. I had my arm around Ellie and to my right was Sherry with her arm around Nikki. In between Sherry and me was Jesus with his arms around both Sherry and me. I was not above Sherry and we weren't above the girls. We were a family working side by side with God nurturing us. Instead of a hierarchy, I saw us as a team, each playing our part.

As I began to serve my family, I noticed that I felt good about myself and that was a new feeling. My self-image as an angry man was destructive to any good feelings toward myself. Now, I found a sense of pleasure in doing well for others, especially my family. As Abraham Lincoln said, "When I do bad, I feel bad. When I do good, I feel good. That is my religion." Being on the better side of that coin was a new and joyful experience.

In the writing I mentioned earlier, the author goes on and says,

> Husbands, love your wives, just as Christ (Jesus) also loved the church and gave himself up for her…. So husbands ought also to love their own wives as their own bodies. He who loves his own wife loves himself; for no one ever hated his own flesh, but nourishes and cherishes it (emphasis added).

What I never understood, in all the years I was angrily criticizing my wife, was I was also destroying my own happiness. Whoever said, "If you want a happy life, have a happy wife," was exactly on target. I did not understand this point of view. For years I saw my happiness based on getting Sherry to do exactly what I wanted.

One of the ways I destroyed my family was upsetting the normal course of communication with Sherry. In a family, there are three means by which spouses respond with one another.
1. *Adult to adult*
2. *Parent to parent*
3. *Child to child*

In the first instance, we speak *adult to adult* about how to spend money, house repairs, school, meals, vacations, chores, and whatever else that goes into the business of leading a family. I compare this to co-workers creating a successful business. You are partners cooperating to produce a winning product or service. If you have a difference of opinion on how to be successful, then you work to resolve the conflict in a healthy manner.

When dealing with children, we speak *parent to parent* about how to discipline, love, raise, and nourish them. In this type of communication, agreement is essential. Imagine if one parent is a harsh disciplinarian and the other parent holds back from correcting the child. They don't try to come into agreement with one another. I was raised in such a family and it took decades to overcome the resentment I felt for the confusing manner in which I was raised.

In the final example we communicate *child to child*. Every adult has a child within them that needs to play. Tickling, laughing together, playing games, and just being funny are all examples of spouses expressing childlike play.

In my life with Sherry, I often would speak to her, not as an equal partner, but as a parent to a child. I would come home from work and find something I didn't like, and then correct her as a parent over a child. I was the authority and she must do what I want. My behavior made her feel not as a valued adult, but rather as a small child being put down. Imagine the pain she felt for being treated as one of our daughters instead of as my wife.

Consider Sherry desiring to complete her master's degree, and my reaction is to speak down to her for even pondering such a decision based on our finances. I was no different than an angry father speaking down to a child who wants money to go to the movies. On the opposite side, think of Sherry talking to me about a problem with her car, but all I want to do is tickle her. Instead of talking as an adult, I am playing like a child.

What made my behavior even worse was that I was striking directly into the heart of Sherry and her sense of being loved. The five love languages are time spent together, acts of service, words of affirmation, gift giving, and physical touch. Each of us has specific "languages of love" that strike close to our identity. In Sherry's case, she felt loved the most by having acts of service done for her and by hearing words of affirmation. I offered neither. I practiced the languages that made *me* feel loved, which are time spent together and physical touch. I never took the time or the energy to express love to her in the ways she understood and appreciated. In fact, I did the opposite.

I angrily criticized Sherry for the housekeeping, for her use of money, for having values and beliefs that were different than mine, for her relationship with God, for her parenting skills, for her family members, and for her failure to understand at all times what I was trying to communicate to her.

Furthermore, I demanded that she consult me on decisions. I vented my anger toward her when I felt anxious or fearful, blaming her for my discomfort. I became angry and defensive when she confronted me over my anger, and made her feel that she shouldn't point out my failures or there would be a price to be paid.

Additionally, Sherry had been asking me for a long period of time to paint the front door and a side fence, and to tear down the girls' old tree house and remove our daughters' play house, neither of which they used as they got older. I violated both of her love languages. I did the opposite of affirming with my criticisms and did not carry out her requests for service. But at the same time, I wanted all of her time and expected physical intimacy as much as possible.

When my eyes were opened, I wrote down a list of what Sherry wanted me to do. The tree house came down and the girls' play house was removed. The front door was painted and so was the fence. During our separation I longed for the day when I could bring coffee to Sherry as she was waking up. To this day it is amazing that the simple act of making coffee in the morning and bringing it to her makes her so happy with me. But it makes her feel loved and that is important.

I stopped criticizing her behaviors I didn't like and learned to listen to her without trying to change her mind. I just listened. Additionally, I am still learning to watch how much I tease her. To me teasing means you are paying attention to me and it does not hurt my feelings. Rather, it makes me feel loved. On the other hand, Sherry, because her language is words of affirmation, does not always feel that way. I can tease her for a short time, but after that it must stop before it begins to feel like an attack on her.

None of my bad behaviors, in my attempt to turn Sherry into what I wanted, ever made me happy. I was miserable as I angrily mistreated my family. But when I stopped trying to get my needs met (again, that never worked) and instead focused on meeting my family's needs, I found over time that healing happened. For example, for years I demanded that Sherry consult with me on any decisions so I could feel respected. After I gave that up, she now asks me all the time what I think about decisions. I often tell her that she can do whatever she wants. She doesn't need to ask me. Yet, she now freely asks me about decisions, not because I demand, but because she now wants to. What I wanted, I finally received, but only because I stopped trying to get it from her.

This belief and behavior change, becoming a servant, did not go easily. I felt great fear that serving Sherry would destroy my chances for happiness. I was fearful that life would be Sherry running roughshod over me. I was still looking at life for what I could get out of it. My needs were still most important in my mind.

What made the transformation from being a drill sergeant to a servant occurred by changing the view I had of myself. Prior I saw myself as a failure in life, failure in my career, and failure in my marriage and as a father. However, during a workshop I was challenged to change that view. During a time of meditation, I saw myself standing with a medieval king and his knights. This statement came to me: "I am a noble knight of the King of kings, fearless and at peace." This was radically different from how I had pictured myself previously.

As I considered becoming a servant to Sherry, as long as I saw her as my wife, and me as a leader over her, I could not serve her. She was my possession. She was here to serve me. But when I stopped seeing her as just my wife, and instead saw her as a queen and me as a knight, I realized a great truth. A knight never asks a queen to serve him. Quite the opposite! The knight exists to serve the desires of the queen. And the reason for this is because he loves the queen. His whole desire is to show his love for her by serving her and fulfilling her desires.

Some may question whether I have just switched positions with Sherry now dominate over me. In other words, our relationship is not an equal partnership, is it? Seeing me as a knight and Sherry as my queen does not make her more valuable than me. I still see us as equal partners. This illustration only gave me the idea of what it truly meant to love someone. Just because you serve someone does not make you less important. My wife treats me with far more value than she ever did when I was angry and dominant.

Additionally, becoming a servant to someone, especially someone I had wounded deeply, begins to make amends for the evil I did to her. When Sherry and I were separated, she asked that I sell the house, give her half the money, and then move back to Indiana so we could co-parent our daughters. I saw that giving her half the money was financial equality, but not an act of amends.

To make amends meant that I needed to do more. I destroyed her happiness and destroyed her financially and socially, and ruined her health. So I wrote and told her that if we sold the house, I would ask to keep $3,000 for a medical bill, my clothes, and my musical instruments. The rest from the house sale, along with all the possessions, was hers. I also knew that she had spent thousands of dollars from her retirement account to start her new life in Indiana. Therefore, I promised to do what I could to pay back into her pension as I had the money.

Now you may think that I was in the wrong for giving up almost all my possessions. But think what Sherry and the girls lost by living with me. I took away their peace, security, love, health, finances, and—because of the move—their relationships. Losing my possessions was a mere drop in the bucket for what I had done. One can replace his possessions. It is much harder to replace peace, love, security, and health.

Even though we are now back together in a healthy marriage, I would still give Sherry our possessions if she felt she could no longer live with me. It is a way to make amends. It does not make me lower than Sherry to serve her. It is one way to make amends.

When I saw this picture in my mind, my fear of serving my wife faded away. I would think of Sherry as my queen instead of my possession. I realized I had been in love with Sherry for years, but I did not truly love her. She existed to make me happy (i.e., I'm in love with you), but it was only later that I came to understand that love means laying down your desires to put the other person above yourself. This change in my thinking, over time, brought healing and joy to Sherry and eventually made me feel, not like a failure, but more like a brave knight.

It is very important that I address a confusion that can occur. As a servant leader I am not the boss or authority over Sherry nor do I want her to see me in that manner. I am not trying to be in charge of her by loving means instead of in anger. Being my wife's boss while treating her in kindness just makes her my employee and not a partner in marriage. If I think of someone as my slave but treat them kindly they still are a slave. Jesus did not teach his followers to be slaves to his leadership despite how lovingly he treated them.

The type of leadership I understand as healthy is one in which, without rank or hierarchy, as an equal, I am given this amazing responsibility of influencing my wife's emotions by love. I am not changing the method of anger for love in order for Sherry to do what I want but in a better manner. I serve her so she feels love. That is my goal rather than getting my way.

The idea that male leadership means I am still the boss of her is the exact opposite to my understanding of male leadership. Male leadership, according to Jesus, means positively influence people's emotions by love.

Now someone may ask, "How do you help your children obey if your goal is to serve? How do you have authority over them if all you are is a slave to their desires?"

I realized that discipline is less about punishment and more about teaching. Previously, I saw disciplining my children as inflicting punishment on them for disobeying me. Now I see it as teaching skills with consequences for disobedience, but not for the purpose of punishing them.

Ellie and I found ourselves arguing over her not wanting to pick up a coat belonging to her sister. Initially I remembered incidents of yelling at her and punishing her because I wanted her to suffer pain, but now I wanted to help her instead of punishing her. I sat down at her feet and told her I would listen to her. She told me that she believed that Sherry and I treat her unfairly in relation to her sister. It was very difficult to hear this, but I realized that Ellie's feelings, whether or not I thought they were accurate, were more important than winning an argument or putting Ellie in her place. After I remained calm and listened, Ellie helped clean up.

To navigate through what feels like chaos in my home—with the goal of loving and healing my family in the long run (rather than trying, in the moment, to stop the chaos through anger and control)—is a very peaceful, shameless, and satisfying experience. I don't have all the answers (only a few) on how to help my children, but this new way of thinking and behaving is so much healthier than yelling, threatening, and controlling. Additionally, it is much easier to come up with solutions when I am calm rather than angry.

As I began to understand this radical style of servant leadership, I discovered new ways to be sensitive to others. One day, I was waiting in a paint store as another painter was paying the female store manager for a *quart* of paint. The store policy is to offer to help clients carry their supplies to their vehicles. Without looking at her, the painter told her "to carry the quart" to his car.

Shocked, I looked into her eyes and for less than a second I saw discomfort. Quickly she smiled. "Sure," she said as she carried his tiny purchase to his car. When she returned, I mentioned what I observed. Her response proved that I was correct in how he had treated her. The demeaning treatment he gave her I probably would have missed in the past, but now I have come to realize that, if you pay attention to others, you often can understand what they are thinking. Realizing these insights gives me sensitivity in helping Sherry process through her emotions, and this often helps her feel validated and loved.

When I talk with Sherry, I try to observe her voice in particular, for it tells me a lot about how she is feeling. I can tell if she is worried, upset, angry, or tired. Often I will ask, "What is wrong? You sound different today." She frequently will say nothing is wrong, but if I tell her what I observed she then will explain her feelings to me. In the past, I was upset when my wife or children were feeling bad. I didn't want my life (after a hard day at work) to be troubled with drama. Now, after taking deep breaths and remaining calm, I can proceed by offering comfort to them—often nothing more than saying, "I'm sorry."

Ellie became upset because Sherry had borrowed her car for an errand and Ellie realized she might be late for work. In the past, I was the only one in the house allowed to act angry and upset. No one else was permitted. Now, I realized that Ellie had a right to be upset. I began to suggest a solution of me driving her to work, but she was still angry at not having her car and was telling me why my solutions wouldn't fix the problem. Instead of getting angry, I simply said, "Honey, I'm trying to help you." Those calm words, instead of escalating the problem, began to defuse the situation and within a few minutes Sherry returned with the car.

The atmosphere of my home, and to a great degree the future of my family, is directly related to how I lead. If I lead with anger, control, and selfishness, like a drill sergeant, then my family's lives will be devastated and the marriage will end. Or, I can stop seeing myself as above my family and become a servant leader to my family. If I do, both my wife and children will feel loved and cared for—and I will be blessed with the joy of doing well. I have great power to influence my family for either life or destruction. It is in my hands.

7

Sherry saved our daughters' lives. Friends of ours invited us to raft a river near us. They said they had done it before. Unfortunately, they rafted it in August when the river level was lower and the rapids were calmer. We were rafting in late May. Ellie and Nikki were five and three years old. They, along with Sherry, were in the front of the raft facing backward where I was paddling.

We approached the first white water drop off and Sherry could see my eyes widen. Over we went as she grabbed both girls through their life jacket straps. Icy cold water flooded over the three of them as we shot through the rapids. I was frightened but could look down river and see that there was only one more drop off and then we were through the rough section. Into that rapid we flew.

I don't remember being catapulted off the back of the raft. My memory failed as I shot over the heads of my family. All I remember was coming to the surface of the water 100 feet downstream. Sherry and girls and raft were gone! I tried to swim through the current upstream, but it was too strong.

I saw Ellie's orange life jacket float by me. It was empty.

"God! She's only five! She can't swim!" I knew she was gone.

Moments later my entire family burst through the water sobbing. Sherry still had her arms wrapped through the straps that had been on the back of the girls' life jackets. I swam to them and helped them onto a gravel beach at the base of a cliff. When they finally calmed down, I asked what happened.

Sherry told me that as soon as I flew over their heads they flipped over backward and into a whirlpool. Pulled underwater she kept trying to push the girls to the surface but the force was too strong.

Somehow, in the midst of seeing all three of them drown, she remembered instructions from a life-saving course she had taken. *Whirlpools are always strongest at the top and weakest at the bottom. Let the current take you down and then you can swim out.*

She stopped fighting the current. Down they went toward the bottom. She kicked her legs, swam out and to the top with the girls. If I were the one holding the girls, we would have all drowned. I say that not because I didn't know about whirlpools (which I didn't), but because of an essential difference between how Sherry and I view the world.

Sherry stopped fighting the current and came up with a solution that saved our daughters' lives and hers. I don't view life that way. I fight against problems. I overcome them by force, frustration, and anger. If it doesn't work, then hit it. However, I never could have overcome the force of that whirlpool.

Think of all the adventure movies you have seen. In the majority of them, men respond to problems with force and often with violence. This is seen as the manly way to deal with problems. If something or someone doesn't work in your favor, then hit them—at least verbally, if not physically.

The question I had to answer was, "Aren't there some instances when it is best to angrily control another person?"

Let me first define the word control. I learned there is mutually agreed control and manipulated control. Mutually agreed control is when an employer and employee agree to types of work and payment received. The employer can tell the worker what to do and the worker has agreed to do that work for the agreed price. There is nothing unhealthy with that arrangement.

Manipulated control is when the employer calls the employee after work hours and demands they come back to work or they will be fired. There was nothing in the work agreement about the worker returning to work after their shift is completed. Forcing them to do so out of fear of losing one's job is manipulation.

I walk into a fast food restaurant and ask for a hamburger and fries. The clerk carries out my order. They have agreed to fulfill my request for their pay. That is mutually agreed control. If I demand that they also watch my little children in their play area while I go shopping, well, that is not a mutually agreed arrangement.

Sherry and I made a number of mutually agreed controls in our marriage. I agreed to handle the car repairs. She agreed to provide most of the meal cooking. That is healthy. What is unhealthy is when I angrily try to control her spending for groceries. I wanted her to behave in a certain way or I would punish her with my anger, disapproval, disregard, and silence. She didn't agree to be treated in such a manner. That is manipulated control in which I used anger to force my desires.

So the question becomes: Isn't it sometimes necessary to angrily control my family? What if my wife hurts me? What if she offends me? Don't I have a right to put her in her place?

Before I could correctly answer that tough question, I had a lot more to learn.

Angry control means my family is my possession. Have you ever seen the cartoon image of a cave man with a club pulling his wife by her hair back to the cave? She is his possession. He can treat her as he wishes. To treat Sherry with angry control means that I can treat her in ways I would never treat a client (or stranger). With clients I am polite, courteous, and helpful to their needs. At home, however, I treated my wife with utter disrespect. Why? Because I thought I could get away with it. She belongs to me and I can behave the way I want. She is my possession.

Yet who wants to be treated as a possession instead of as a person in a loving relationship? And who wants to be seen as an emotional caveman to his family? My family is not my possession. They are a gift from God to me and I am responsible to protect their well-being.

Angry control works but destroys my family in the process. I was asked, "What did you get out of being angry with someone? There had to be something you got out of it." There were two results that gave me reasons to be angry.

One, I got my way. Sherry manipulated her life to keep me calm. Nikki, our youngest, became a people pleaser so I wouldn't erupt in anger. My family danced on tiptoes to avoid a scene with me.

Two, when I didn't get my way, then I was able to vent my rage and frustration for being hindered from my desires. In a word, I was a dictator. The only problem with being a dictator was that my family's personalities were being destroyed by my behavior. Nikki and Ellie both had issues and Sherry thought she was losing her mind. What attracted me to Sherry was her vivacious personality. The more I controlled her, however, the less of her delightful personality showed.

Sherry and I fought often. The girls hated when we went to counseling because there was so much hurt and pain afterward. There was little emotional intimacy between us. Finally, my family had enough. They left me. To put it another way, angry control worked for a while and then it destroyed my family and my relationship with them. Eventually, there were far more problems with being angry than not being angry.

Angry control is always worse than the offense I am fighting. Have you ever noticed a fight break out on a children's playground? Someone cuts in front of someone or says a hurtful word. What does the offended child do? He might push the other person. That person pushes back harder. The offended person steps up the game and punches the other person in the nose. Now a fight is on.

What I see in this scenario is that the resulting behavior is always worse than the original offense. The increase in violence is the nature of angry control. This behavior is not limited to children. Consider road rage incidents. Someone cuts in front of another person. No one is hurt but an offense is caused. Disrespect has occurred. The offender must be punished. Does the other driver cut in front of him? No. Instead, he might try to force him off the road or ride his bumper to scare him. In extreme cases he pulls out a gun and shoots the person. Angry control is always worse than the original offense.

One day Ellie was angry with Nikki. My response was to tell her that she could pack a suitcase and go find a family to live with if ours was so terrible. My goal was to control her behavior. I did it by angry and extreme statements that hurt my family far more than Ellie's drama.

In my marriage, I often manipulated Sherry over our finances. I confronted her about spending more on groceries than we had budgeted. I would insist she justify the additional expense, making her feel like a child. A calm person would have talked with her and seen where we could cut back on the budget to make up for the extra food expense. But my response was not calm. I was critical and demeaning. I didn't even think of asking how we could solve the budget problem. If she did something I felt was wrong or not wise, I would react with a response far worse than her behavior. The end result was our separation cost us exceedingly far more than any extra expense for groceries.

Angry control cannot overcome the wrong or offense. Angry control of my family did not change the behaviors. I wanted Sherry to pay more attention to me. I wanted the girls to keep the house clean. None of that happened. My anger did not change their behaviors for the long run. There had to be another way to deal with offense, hurt, and fear other than fighting it.

When Sherry rescued our daughters, she did not fight against the current. Instead she recognized where it was the weakest. I discovered this while working in Hawaii many years ago. I met a group of gang members who hung out near where I worked. Closing the shop one night I heard angry shouts. Down the street the gang members were beating up a drunken tourist. He was lying in the street. Blood ran from his head. I stepped in front of them and asked them to stop. "Look! He's a stupid tourist. He is injured. Don't hurt him anymore," I said.

Immediately, I was surrounded by all six gang members. "Do you want some of this?" the leader threatened.

"No. Look guys. You know me. I work right over there."

"Then get back to work!"

"Okay, but don't hit him anymore."

They ignored the wounded tourist, walked away, and the tourist stumbled off in another direction.

Now in this situation, I used the weakest link in these gang members' armor. I appealed to the fact that they knew me. We had some sort of relationship. I wasn't going to try to hurt them. They were in no danger from me. This was control based on no harm to them. I got what I wanted: they left the tourist, and they got what they wanted: they told me what to do and I didn't resist them.

I could have ploughed into all six of them. Since they were so much smaller than me, I could have grabbed the leader by the throat, strangled him, and threatened to kill him if the others didn't back off. I saw this in another fight they had with one guy. He took down the leader and most of the other gang members left him alone. But because I didn't angrily control them, they walked away at peace with me. If I had fought them, they would have eventually gotten back at me. In fact, later that evening a much older gang member confronted me as if I had fought them. I told him what had happened and he left.

When Sherry offends me, reacting to her in a similar manner will only continue the hurt and pain. What changes the spirit of a wife is not increased anger but a loving response. Feeling loved is where my wife is softest toward me.

Angry control destroys love in my family. As I mentioned in the previous chapter, I accomplish more in family leadership by my influence than by commands. So, if I believe I have a right to angrily control my family, then by what kind of spirit am I influencing my family? Not by love, but rather anger and domination. How can I have a loving family if the attitude with which I treat them is unloving? Whatever the attitude of my heart is will influence my family. If my attitude is one of love, then that spirit influences my family positively.

My family and I were riding in the car. Ellie and Nikki were bickering with one another. Sherry was upset with them and I could feel the urge to angrily take control. The tension increased my anxious feelings. I felt powerless to have peace in our family. I wanted to command them to be quiet.

Instead, I prayed that God would help me stay calm, and not hurt anyone's feelings, even though I was emotionally uncomfortable with the drama. I remembered times exploding in frustration with the fighting and then taking control by telling everyone to "knock it off!"

This time I realized I didn't need to meet my needs for peace and quiet. Rather, I could think of my family's feelings. Sherry had been nervous and uptight the past few days. Ellie and Nikki were just girls. They were not adults. I could help them all by remaining calm and peaceful. I chose to behave in a spirit opposite to the current attitude in the car.

I kept my mouth shut and stayed quiet.

The result was that the tension in the car deescalated and there was peace. Had I behaved in an angry controlling manner, it would have only increased the tension and pain in the car. It would not have fixed the lack of love we were experiencing. It would have made it far worse. It always does.

Angry control assumes I am God and can judge and bring punishment to my family. In medieval times, knights were baptized into the Christian faith prior to embarking on their crusades. When they were baptized, they would hold their swords above the water. The idea was that they would surrender their lives to God, but they would do what they wanted with their swords. The bloodshed of the crusades demonstrated the horribleness of that belief. When I assume I can judge and punish my family, as only God should, I enter not a world of God's goodness but one of evil.

Wrongly believing God has given me rights as a man to punish my family assumes that I have God's mindset. I believe I think like God and know the intentions and motivations of my family members. Such arrogance on my part demonstrates not God's heart of love, but something far more selfish and horrific in nature. It is not God who coerces me to punish my family's failures. That belief comes from evil.

When I saw Sherry and the girls back East, Sherry asked if I would take Christmas presents to her family. I was very nervous. I had destroyed my family and ruined my marriage. I did not want to meet my mother-in-law. After flying home, I knocked on their door and a nephew opened it. I quickly handed him the presents, wished him a Merry Christmas, and turned to go.

"Who is that?" my mother-in-law called from inside the house.

"It's Uncle Brent!"

"Tell him to come in here," she replied.

"I need to go," I said.

"I want to see him," she gently said.

I stood on their front porch sobbing while she held me in her arms and forgave me. She showed me more of the nature of God than any punishment or judgment ever would. If I want to act like God, then I need to forgive the offenses of my family instead of angrily punishing and judging them.

Is angry control of my family ever correct? No. Not if my goal is to help foster a loving family. What about Jesus? Didn't he make a whip out of rope and chase the money changers out of the temple? He obviously was angry and with force made others do what they did not want. Isn't that angry control?

Jesus, according to the Bible, is the Son of God. If anyone knows how to be angry and not do evil, it would be him. The last I checked, I'm not the Son of God. I don't know how to exercise angry control and not bring harm to others and to God's work. I don't know anyone else who is the one and only Son of God. Those who claim to be God's unique Son either end up in mental institutions or prison, or at least they should.

Therefore, it is safe to say that angry control of my family is never correct. If I want to confront wrongs in my family, I need to approach them with love and forgiveness.

8

Nothing else has worked. Why not try something new?

I slammed the phone. I had been talking with Sherry regarding a problem at work and she wasn't solving it or, at the very least, wasn't soothing my emotional pain. Frustrated, I wanted her to feel guilty for not relieving my stress and frustration. I wanted her to help me feel better. I wanted her to make my life a happier time. When she didn't, I slammed the phone in anger at both her and the problem.

The owner of a company is upset that his latest shipment of product is delayed by a truckers' strike. Angry, he expresses his frustrations at his executives. Feeling unduly chastised by the owner, they take out their frustration on the foremen. The foremen aren't happy now. They snap at the factory workers. Now, they aren't happy.

Upon arriving home from the job, the workers feel miserable and refuse to show any concern for their wives, who are just getting home from their own jobs. The wives chew out the children for the messy house and one of the kids kicks the dog.

The dog thinks, *What did I do?*

Far more times than I can imagine, Sherry would look at me and ask, "What did I do that makes you so angry at me?" I never could come up with a justifiable reason or excuse. I was just mad at her for not fixing my problems.

It became very clear in my marriage that I had a deep belief, one that I was not very conscious of, that Sherry should meet my needs and make me happy. If I was anxious, fearful, or worried, it was her job to make me feel secure and safe. While I never have thought of her as a "mother" to me, that was what I wanted her to accomplish for me. Help me feel safe.

As our marriage continued and my anger exploded time and again, I had to stop trying to make Sherry meet my needs for security, safety, and resolution of problems. I needed to learn to do something new. That required some big changes in my core beliefs. Yet the truths I learned soon made sense to me.

So, what did I learn?

Sherry is not responsible for my happiness. This is so contrary to why people get married, but it is true. How in the world can another person reach inside my mind and change the way I respond to life? Most people barely understand their own behaviors and have little ability to change what they do know. How is it possible that I expected Sherry to change what is wrong in me so I can be happy? Yet that is what I wanted her to do.

I married Sherry because she made me feel like no other person in the world. I was excited to be with her. I wanted to live my life with her. But she does not have the ability to change what is wrong in my life. She cannot fix my problems. I married a wife, not a psychologist. She may understand why I have anxiety, but she cannot change it. Making her responsible to heal me was a frightening load to place on her. She is not responsible for my life.

The idea that people are responsible for my happiness can extend far beyond my wife. Often I would be irritated with my employees and their behaviors. Fortunately, after going through recovery, I learned that my happiness does not depend on them. One evening a business owner called to say that my employee never showed up to prepare his building for painting. I felt anxiety, panic, and dread. This employee's behavior made our company look bad and put us off schedule. I prayed that I would not be hurtful to him in dealing with the situation.

I considered that perhaps he was ill and, still being young, decided to tell me in the morning. When we met, however, he told me he had done the work. The owner was mistaken. The owner was relieved that I hadn't corrected my employee, and my worker was happy he wasn't in trouble. None of this would have occurred had I still believed that other people are responsible to make me happy and, if they don't, then they will suffer my wrath.

Sherry is not designed to meet my needs that only God can meet. I would think that common sense would have taught me this truth. But honestly, many years ago I tried to make Sherry into something she wasn't. She often would complain to me that I had her on some sort of a pedestal. I simply didn't know the real Sherry—only my faulty image of her.

When Sherry and I reconnected years later, I would argue with her about what she liked or preferred in life. She would look at me as if I had a screw loose. She would tell me something about herself and I would respond with "that's not how you feel." I would then try to convince her that she felt and thought exactly what I needed from her. She argued that she was not like that at all. I would argue that she was (based on my false image of her).

Because I expected Sherry to make me happy and she could not (nor is any woman able to do that for a man), I made her miserable with my expectations. Worse, I failed to trust God for my deepest needs. As a result, I continued in anger and self-focus.

What I expected of Sherry was similar to driving down the road, seeing the bridge is out, and then speeding up the car so you can fly across the chasm. The resulting crash? That's what eventually happened in my marriage. I was trying to get Sherry to do what she was not made to do. She was not designed to meet my needs. She was designed to point out where I was not right in my behavior. My response should have been to accept her rebuke and turn to God to change me.

Only God can meet my needs for security, safety and provision. I did not trust God for my finances, my transformation, our daughters' healing, and reconciliation with Sherry. Instead of trusting God, I worried over money, complaining about Sherry's purchases. I preached at my daughters and tried to change their behaviors with my words. I worried that if I didn't change my own behaviors, then Sherry would not reconcile with me.

I attended a public AA meeting with a friend. The speaker talked about all that alcohol had stolen from him. I realized that my unwillingness to trust God—and all of the anger, control, and selfishness—had taken my wife, daughters, and previous career away from me. I heard myself ask what anger, control, and lack of trusting God had ever done for me in the long run. Why not let go of those behaviors and see if things don't change for the better? Certainly doing what I have always done had produced nothing but pain, heartache, and misery for Sherry, Ellie, Nikki, and me.

So, I began to put my trust in God. This was put to the test rather quickly. My parents were elderly and, due to their health conditions, needed to move into an assisted living facility. We met with the administrator of a facility they liked and were promised a room at a specific price.

Prior to them moving in, I received a voicemail from the facility saying that the situation had changed and the price had been raised nearly five hundred percent. My initial response was fear, hopelessness, worry, and a sense of injustice. I felt powerlessness. I prayed and waited to call back when I was not angry.

I explained that while this massive price change was probably not their fault—since someone who owned the facility had made the decision—it was wrong to break their promise to two elderly people living on a fixed income. The administrator agreed with me that this was wrong to do. Soon the decision was reversed and my parents have lived in this facility for years at a price they can afford.

Not becoming angry and controlling with the staff, but rather calmly pointing out the injustice and trusting God to change their hearts, was a new behavior in my life. I needed to do the same practice of trust in God with my marriage, finances, and the overall transformation of my beliefs and behaviors. As I have said before, this was not easy.

One morning I woke with great fear. I feared I could not change. I considered myself an unredeemable human incapable of becoming a loving, selfless person. The horror of thinking that I could not be saved, that I was trapped into wickedness, gripped me. I feared I would spend eternity in hell. As I fought with these thoughts, I remembered writings from the Bible that gave me hope that God could redeem me, and that I could be transformed from the horrible life I had been living. I had to believe that God would be that merciful to me. I had to believe his word over my fears.

After my family left, I had to realize that my life was in God's hands and not in Sherry's. As I wrote in my journal shortly after they moved away,

> *If I did not see myself in the hand of God; if I did not see my circumstances as being something God is orchestrating; if I did not see this time as being allowed by God, I would panic. If I see Sherry as being in charge, calling the shots, forcing me to do what she wants, I would be in fear... But if I accept my circumstances as God being in control, then I have peace for I trust him. I have hurt and (at times) broken-heartedness, but I know I have the Lord.*

My counselor talked with me about relaxing in the knowledge that God is in control of my past and my future. I am to live in the moment. So often with Sherry and the girls, I would worry about the future and feel guilty over the past. But as the weeks and months carried on, I learned to live moment by moment, alone with God. I didn't need Sherry or anyone else to meet my needs for love, security, and acceptance.

A little over a year after Sherry and the girls left, she called and said they were moving back home. She was not ready to live with me, but we could co-parent the girls.

They moved home and I moved out. One night she asked me to go to dinner with her. It was terrible. What could I possible talk about with someone who was still legally my wife, but emotionally divorced from me? I kept thinking that perhaps putting our family back together was a very bad idea. Fortunately, both Sherry and I trusted God, though we really didn't know how things were going to work out.

Two more years went by and Sherry and I spent time with the girls, went on vacations, and did family events. We just didn't live together. There was an increasing emotional closeness, but Sherry still didn't trust me.

Then I fell twenty-two feet off a house.

My ladder, sitting on the first story roof, slipped and I flipped upside down. I hit the back of my neck on the roof, bounced in the air as if off a trampoline, did another flip, and crashed upside down into a tree. From there I fell to the ground.

A surgeon was sewing my left ear back on when I came to in the trauma unit. I could not twist my head. There was a tight collar from my shoulders to my chin. I asked what happened and they told me I had broken my neck. Specifically, I had broken the C-2 and C-5 vertebrae. Additionally, I fractured my upper back. All I could say was, "Look! I can move my fingers and toes!" Every question they asked me, I answered, "Look! I can move my fingers and toes!" Sherry looked at the nurse, who shook her head and quietly explained that people with bad concussions usually speak nonsense.

When I was released from the hospital, Sherry took me home. For the first time in years I slept in the same bed with my wife. I should have been very grateful. According to the doctors, when you sever your spine at the C-2 vertebrae, it paralyzes your heart and lungs. It is called the hangman's break. When you sever your spine at the C-5 vertebrae, it makes you a quadriplegic. I was alive. I could walk and talk. I should have been very thankful. I wasn't.

I was mad at God. I had no insurance and—for the days in the trauma unit—I now owed $30,000. I couldn't work, was losing money, and now was horribly in debt.

My question to God was: *Why didn't you just keep the ladder on the roof?* Yet God had spared my life and saved me from paralysis. *Still, how could it be so hard to just hold the ladder in place?* I kept most of this to myself. Many months later I shared my feelings with Sherry.

"Brent, I never had re-bonded with you. I didn't know if I ever would be close to you again. When you were injured, it caused my heart to emotionally bond with you. I realized how deeply I had come to care about you." In that moment I thanked God for the accident. The accident and hospital bills were nothing compared to having my wife love me once again. I am grateful.

The past few years I have learned more about trusting God. My life is a process of transformation, and I am not perfect in any of them, but I do know the validity of these truths as I practice them.

One truth is that trusting God means I no longer angrily control or manipulate other people. I trust that God is in control and I don't need to be. This practice, particularly of not angrily controlling Sherry or our daughters, has given great freedom to our family. Not long after Sherry and the girls left, two different women told me, in essence, "If you husbands would let us be free, and not try to control us, you would have no idea how much love we would show you!" I have found this statement right on the mark, especially with Sherry. I am amazed at how much love she expresses to me these days.

Two is letting go of methods to medicate my pain. Alcohol, marijuana, pornography, television, and daydreaming are common means to ease pain but, if I use any of them, it indicates I am not trusting God to heal my hurts. Pornography did nothing to help heal the chasm between Sherry and me. Ditto watching television for hours after work. I finally realized TV wasn't helping me become a less angry person. It was only easing my suffering.

As the years went by and Sherry and I had not reconciled, I began to daydream about leaving the country after our daughters went off to college. I imagined moving to Puerto Rico and living my life away from people who knew how terrible I had been. *Start a new life.* I found great comfort in that dream until I realized it was just a way of easing the pain of my loneliness. I saw that I needed to face my pain and trust God to change and heal me.

Three is waiting for God to work. I waited three and a half years before Sherry trusted me enough to invite me home for good. They were not enjoyable years to wait, but God did what I did not think was possible. Sherry was rightfully so angry and mistrustful of me that it seemed impossible to reconcile. However, as my heart became soft and loving toward her, she was drawn to me. As a woman, her emotions were designed to respond to how she was treated. As I treated her with love, she eventually found the ability to respond back in love.

Four is giving thanks in the midst of suffering. I had to learn not to return to anger and rage because life was dragging on with little sense of redemption between Sherry and me. I had to learn to be grateful for every blessing of God, even when it did not look like Sherry and I would ever reconcile. Giving thanks, even in hard times, keeps my heart from becoming angry. I still need to learn this. I don't want to swear at God about my circumstances. Instead, I want my first reaction to be one of thanks for his presence in my life.

Five is asking God to show me what I need to do. I asked him if I could change. I asked God if my family would be saved. I took instruction from others. I also heard God speak truth into my mind. I studied books of other peoples' experiences like mine that helped guide me. I read portions of the Bible, again and again, to discover how to trust God and live without anger.

Six is obeying what God teaches me. There was no need to tell God I trust him if I refuse to do what he tells me. This meant I had to guard not just my words and actions to others, but also my thoughts. As upset as I was that Sherry took the girls away from me, I could not allow thoughts of anger to fester in my mind. I had to guard against ideas of revenge against Sherry for leaving me. She would often call for money for their support, needing something mailed from home to her, or telling me about decisions she had made. I needed to obey God by fulfilling her requests. Additionally, I needed to control my sexual thoughts and not allow them to go wherever they wanted. I needed to obey God with what I thought about.

This became front and center after my family moved home. I had been learning a tremendous amount from my recovery program, but now I had a daily exercise of putting these behaviors into practice. Both of our daughters were angry with Sherry for moving them away from home and friends for a year. They were disrespectful and disobedient to her. Many times I tried to stop them, behaving angry and controlling, saying words that were hurtful to the girls.

But over time, I ignored what my angry thoughts said and asked God what to do. Often he would tell me to be quiet. This was so difficult to obey. I wanted to say what was in my mind. But I obeyed. That way, the girls weren't wounded by my words as in the past. I had peace in my heart. Finally, after my emotions had calmed down, I was able to talk with the girls about a better way to speak to their mom. They agreed with me.

Please don't think I now have this hardwired. I am still learning to obey God.

Seven, I learned that in trusting God, I have to be willing to suffer through painful circumstances as I wait for God to work. I don't like pain. Never have. But I had to learn to suffer and still trust God. Had I decided somewhere in those years of separation that I just couldn't bear the waiting anymore, and had moved to Puerto Rico, then I wouldn't be married today.

Furthermore, my daughters would have had more pain to deal with. Finally, I would have never learned the blessings that can come to those who trust and wait on God.

Trusting God was new for me, but nothing else had worked. I decided to try it, and it worked.

9

I was single for forty-three years. I despised aloneness. So, I adapted to the situation. I started long-term dating relationships with women—not to be married someday, but solely so I wouldn't be lonely. Over the years I was in long-term dating relationships with two wonderful women. I hurt them deeply by using them for my own purposes of companionship. I was selfish and unloving to them. Both of them were terribly wounded by me.

After the second relationship ended, I found myself sitting on the wall of a monastery graveyard. I saw how I had used both women to take away my loneliness. I realized I had never trusted or depended on God with this area of my life.

If I surrendered this part of my life to God, I was certain that I would be kept alone and lonely the rest of my life. I looked at all the dead monks buried in the ground below me. I knew I would die alone like them.

Still, I said yes to God. I told him I would date only who he said to date.

A month later I moved out of town to a new job in a big city. I would walk the streets at night telling God how lonely I was. I had no friends. My life was miserable.

Then one evening at a banquet I met a beautiful single woman. We talked long after the banquet was finished. We left only because the custodians were sweeping. She was wonderful in conversation. As I got in my car I knew I would call her and ask her out.

"Don't you dare."

The thought was extremely clear in my mind. "Do not date her." I argued with God. I told him how lonely I was. Yet, the word was clear. "No!"

Over the next few weeks I asked God if I could just have lunch with her. Coffee? Anything? Always, the answer was no.

So, for the first time in my life, I obeyed God in what he told me to do with relationships. I trusted him even though I was very lonely. It seemed that the idea of dying like a monk was coming true.

Two months went by. My office intercom rang. "There is a call for you," the secretary said.

It was Sherry. After almost twelve years since last seeing her, Sherry called to see if we could start all over again. Had I started a relationship with the other woman, I would have once again broken someone's heart. Trusting God meant I had to go through the process of obedience even though it meant suffering through painful times. But it brought a wonderful transformation from singleness to marriage.

During my marital separation, I again had to practice a willingness to go through suffering to achieve transformation of my character. There is perhaps a better word than suffering. It's discipline. If I was going to change my beliefs and behaviors, I needed to discipline myself to change, including living through the consequences of what I had done to my family. That meant being alone, scared, and never knowing when I might see my children again.

There were three agonizing areas I had to live through so I could experience transformation. One was the loss of my family, of course. Two was the shame I experienced. Three was the discipline of allowing my beliefs and behaviors to be changed. None of these were pain-free, but I had to walk through all three in order to change.

I believe that most everything in life requires discipline in order for us to succeed. As a toddler, I disciplined myself to walk even though I fell often and got hurt. As a boy, I disciplined my body and mind to play sports. As I got older, I disciplined my intellect in school so I could learn. I disciplined myself to work so I could make a living. As a teenager, I worked in a food factory. My last position was to clean out the sausage kitchen. I worked alone cleaning from 7 p.m. till 3:30 a.m. I hated that summer, but it taught me how to work through tough times as I prepared for college. If I do not discipline myself, then I fail to grow and succeed.

I found it is especially important to discipline myself in the area of character traits. I often failed to see how immature I was. Sherry tried to warn me about my anger and control. I sensed God speaking to me to alter my ways. I knew I had a problem, but I did not discipline myself to change.

I want to stress this point: I was warned by my wife and God to change my life, but I ignored those warnings. If I had done the opposite, I could have saved so much future pain for my family and me. But I did not discipline myself to obey. So, there was one last way to open my eyes to the issues in my character.

Pain!

When Sherry and the girls left, I sensed pain in ways previously unknown to me. I also felt deep fear and anxiety I had not experienced in years. I knew I needed to do something. I went into a recovery program for more than two years. I attended an emotionally difficult workshop. I took personal counseling. I sought after God to change my life. I kept a journal to record what I was learning.

The recovery program and counseling cost money I barely had. Still, I disciplined my mind, money, and time to change my character. None of these disciplines was enjoyable. Especially since Sherry did not come running back to me. But if I was going to grow as a person, I needed to discipline myself—through the pain.

One of the areas where I needed to discipline myself was through the consequences of losing my family. I missed my daughters terribly. At first I believed Sherry and the girls would return home after summer vacation if I would go into treatment. In August, Sherry contacted me and said that they were just getting started in counseling and needed more time. She was putting the girls into public school and they would continue to live back East.

I thought often of contacting a judge and legally ordering Sherry to bring our daughters back to Oregon to live with me. I certainly had that legal right and Sherry was aware that I might act in that manner. However, I realized that I did not want a custody fight with Sherry, that pulling the girls between us would damage them further, and finally, that with working all day long I had no way to take care of two little girls. I realized, as horrible as it was to not see my daughters, this was the price I had to pay for how I had treated them and Sherry. I did not know when I would ever see them again. Therefore, I had to trust God to open the opportunity to be with them at the correct time.

Three months after they left, Sherry told me the counselor wanted more time with the girls before I could visit. Therefore, I would be unable to attend Nikki's birthday in September. Could I come at Christmas? This meant a total of six months until I would see them again. I was devastated, but said yes. Over the year I visited my family three times. Every time I had to leave my daughters and get on a plane, felt like a nightmare, but it was one I had created by my behaviors, and so I had to endure it.

At any time during that first year, when my family lived away from home, I could have given up on saving my marriage, and given up on changing my beliefs and behaviors, and tried to take control of my children. It was tempting. But I knew I had to discipline my life though pain so that hoped-for good could come.

In addition, I had to discipline myself through the shame of my past behaviors. Multiple times people would ask, "Where are Sherry and the girls? I haven't seen them." I wanted to tell the questioner that they were visiting family…for a very long time. Instead, it was humiliating to admit to others that I had driven my family away because of my anger and control. But if I was going to change, I needed to be honest and tell the truth, regardless of what others thought of me.

I remember telling one of my friends what had happened. His response was, "Why did you treat your children that way?" He was not smiling when he asked. Furthermore, I had to go to classes with other men who, in my initial opinion, had treated their wives much worse than I had. I thought I was not as bad as they were. It was embarrassing to be associated with them.

I attended weekly classes and weekly counseling. The class leaders were polite but they took how I treated my family seriously. They did not make it easy on me. I would have done anything other than have to face the shame of dealing with the ugliness of my life. The class homework required me to deal with the horror of how selfish I was. Yes, I could have quit.

If I had quit, however, all that's good in my life would vanish and I would not be writing this book today. I would still continue to be angry and controlling, looking for some way out of the mess of my life, without disciplining myself. Holding myself accountable to my group made me face the mess of my life. It was not fun having leaders and classmates confront the bad behaviors I had to share with the class. It was humiliating. But disciplining myself through the shame allowed me to come to a place where I knew I did not want to be angry and controlling any longer. I was willing to change. I was desperate to change. And I wouldn't settle for anything less.

The third area of discipline was allowing my beliefs and behaviors to be changed and to practice those changed behaviors. One of the major disciplines I had to practice was to stop controlling Sherry. This was a major behavior in my life and one I was frightened to stop. This was especially true when she began to make all the decisions for our children: their counseling, schooling, activities, finances, and where they lived. I felt powerless, which was something I hated. I had to restrain myself from taking over control and instead trust that God was powerful enough to work rightly in her life.

I had to discipline my tongue in how I spoke to our daughters, especially when they disobeyed. To be silent when I wanted to angrily correct them—and wait until I had calmed down—was a major effort on my part. I wanted to be in control of them, so giving up trying to control them (so I could help direct them) took lots of discipline.

I had to discipline my tongue outside the family, as well. Sometime after my family returned home, but while we were still separated, a neighbor friend called Sherry. There was an issue between their daughter and one of ours and they wanted to talk about it. Sherry and I went to their house. As soon as we came on their property, the husband stepped out of the house. He looked at me. "We wanted to talk only with Sherry," he informed me.

I was in shock. I wanted to tell him that Sherry's daughter was also my daughter and as her father he could also talk with me. Instead, I said, "Oh. Okay." And then I turned and went home. I had a lot of negative thoughts in my mind. Once again, I was the person no one wanted around. I was just kicked off someone's property. I am not important enough to speak to. I am being controlled. As I said, I had lots of negative thoughts.

The next day the husband called and explained that since Sherry and I were separated, he and his wife didn't want to stir up a conflict in parenting between us. So, they thought it better to just talk with Sherry. I thanked him and we hung up. Had I not disciplined my tongue, and ignored the negative thoughts I had, there is no end to the wrong that could have happened. Discipline is difficult, but it sets the path for goodness in the future. To this day he and I are friends.

Every day I have to discipline myself to continue to think loving thoughts, reject negative thinking, and behave in loving ways to my family. It is much easier than it was (say) eight or nine years ago, but it still requires discipline when I feel like expressing my anger and frustration. But I am glad that I came through the dark days instead of bailing out of the necessary discipline.

I am reminded of a caterpillar that forms a cocoon around itself. That small creature has no idea what all that darkness will produce. It is powerless inside its cocoon. But in the darkness there is transformation. At first, it looks bad. The caterpillar dissolves into DNA soup. Then something beautiful begins to form and eventually a gorgeous butterfly emerges, stretches and dries its wings, and then flies into the air. What was once a crawling creature on the ground becomes a beauty of flight, able to sail through the sky.

The years of separation encompassed lots of darkness. I felt cocooned and often thought of giving up hope. But what was happening was a transformation of character. I just had to discipline myself to walk through the dark days. But along the way I experienced God's mercy.

After my first visit, with no idea of when I might be invited back to see my family, I stepped onto an airplane on Christmas Eve to fly home. I sat next to the window as tears ran down my cheeks, still seeing Nikki crying as I boarded. Eventually, the gentleman next to me asked what I was doing. I talked with him. He kept asking questions. Over the next hour and half I told him about my life, what I was learning through recovery, and ways to change from anger to love.

As we were landing in Denver, I asked him what he did for a living. "I am a psychologist." For an hour and half I was sitting next to a man who helps people by listening to them. As he was leaving the lady next to him turned to me and said, "I will be praying for you and your family." In that moment, I knew that God was still with me. In the midst of the pain, I was still not alone.

10

Sherry and I do not agree on everything. That's good. For years, however, my goal was to win every argument. I had no desire to learn her opinion or motivation. I just wanted to win. I may have learned this from my dad. For almost two years he and I argued over nuclear weapons. My mom would cry out for us to stop fighting.

"We are not arguing," I would shout. "We are debating!"

One night as we debated, my dad said, "That is the best argument I have heard you make." I continued to argue with him. Suddenly I realized what he had told me.

"What?" I asked.

"That is the best argument I have heard you make over these years."

"You agree with me?" I asked in shock.

"I have always agreed with you. I just wanted to see you defend your opinion correctly."

At that point I did not know whether to high five him for agreeing with me or strangle him for all the emotional pain he had caused me over the previous two years.

What I did know for certain was the idea of arguing to win. If Sherry and I did not agree, then I did not care to learn her opinion, perspective, or motivation. I only wanted to change her mind to agree with me.

I have several reasons why I behaved this way. Again, I was convinced that in a disagreement, the goal was to win. To mentally dominate the other person was the idea—to prove that I was correct. Another reason was my false belief that for Sherry and me to be close to one another, we needed to agree on most everything. After all, when you agree with someone else, you feel a sense of closeness to them. Therefore, I concluded that Sherry and I must agree. Finally, I was selfish. My ideas were right and therefore Sherry must be wrong when she disagreed with me. However, very quickly I discovered we had differences, and I don't mean where to squeeze the toothpaste tube.

I do not use alcohol. With my type of personality, the use of alcohol would, as one person told me, "turn you into an angry drunk." I am already angry. Alcohol would only make it worse. On the other hand, Sherry does not see a problem for people to drink in moderation. When I found this out I was shocked. How could we be close to one another when something that is so foreign to me is permissible for her?

My solution was to try to change her mind.

My underlying belief was that perspectives were either right or wrong. If you do not agree with my perspective, then you are wrong. At no point did I even consider trying to understand her perspective on why she believes what she does. If I did ask her such questions, it was only so I could interrupt and argue against her opinion. I had no ability to truly listen to her and learn. All I wanted to accomplish was to win the argument.

Sherry would often sing a once popular song lyric to me: "There ain't no good guy, there ain't no bad guy. There's only you and me and we just disagree." This idea was foreign to me. My opinion was good and right. If hers differed, it was wrong or bad, or both.

I can only imagine what it must have been like for Sherry. Every time we did not agree, I refused to listen to her and instead attempted, often with anger, to smash her ideas. I am reminded of the Whack a Mole game where little creatures stick their heads out of holes, and you smash them down with a hammer as fast as you can. I wanted to smash her differing ideas. No wonder she felt as if her self-image was destroyed by marrying me.

When I finally stopped trying to control the world around me, I saw I needed to truly listen to Sherry's perspective on life—without trying to change her and without necessarily agreeing with her. Furthermore, I could do both and still be close to her. In fact, when I stopped controlling her, we eventually became much closer.

There were a number of steps I took to learn how to listen to others and validate their perspectives.

I stopped talking so much. I have report cards from early grade school. They all have the same teacher remarks: "Brent talks too much in class." I did not see a problem. However, as I became an adult, I discovered why I talk so much. I wanted people to pay attention to me. It built my self-image. When I came into a room I would manipulate the conversation so everyone was paying attention to me. If that did not work, then I would get one on one with someone and talk to them. The whole goal was to be noticed.

Nowadays I will sometimes notice how much I talk at parties. If I think I talked too much, I will ask Sherry. She is able to give me good input on whether I was dominating the conversation or only adding in what was appropriate.

I have a friend who makes you feel like a million dollars. I believe the reason is that he invests his time in you. He listens and pays attention and makes you feel like you are the most valuable person in the world. On the other hand, there are people who talk only about themselves and express no interest in your world. I want to be like my friend. I do not want to continue to dominate in conversation. The way out of that is for me to be quiet and listen.

I decided to learn what others thought. I needed to have an interest in other people besides what they could do for me. I know people who behave in the latter manner. They make me feel like the only reason they spend time with me is when they benefit. Otherwise, I never hear from them. This is not an easy task for me. Being selfless means I have to practice wanting to learn about others. I do this best by asking questions of other people rather than looking for an opportunity to tell my stories. It is also helpful to remind myself that life is not about me. I behave best when I give my attention to others. Looking to further my interests in a conversation does not bode well.

I learned to wait in conversation. Recently, someone told me a great story about themselves. Immediately I thought of a similar situation. I wanted to interrupt and tell them my story. If we had similar stories, then we would be closer to one another. We thought or did something alike. My problem was that I just took the attention away from them and turned it onto myself. But if I comment appropriately about their story and then wait in silence, they will continue to tell me more about themselves. I just have to wait.

I stopped interrupting people when they were talking. I grew up with relatives who all talked at once. There was a lot of noise, but I am not certain how many of us really listened to one another. We were all busy telling our own stories. One of the worst ways to control another person is by interrupting. I will never learn about others' perspectives if I interrupt. It makes people, especially Sherry, stop talking. If I want to grow close to another person, I need to let them talk.

At a dinner party I sat next to someone who had offended me in the past. Immediately I thought of how I could get out of the conversation or turn the attention onto myself. Realizing this was an unhealthy behavior, I began to be quiet and listen. For forty-five minutes the man spoke about his life. While this was not enjoyable, I didn't die by not interrupting him and I actually learned a bit about him. Furthermore, it brought some healing between him and me. I found that I could give my attention to others and not feel left out simply by ignoring some desire within me to be noticed. Conversely, I found that not talking, but truly listening, actually brings others closer to me.

I listened for their perspective without becoming defensive or argumentative. A friend gave me a very good word as I was leaving to visit my family back East. She sensed that a spirit of worthlessness was in me—and that Sherry would never be able to share her hurts, anger, and pain with me and be validated, listened to, and apologized to—if I was under such a spirit. She felt I would be defensive and become focused on my feelings instead of Sherry's. I had no idea how important her counsel would become to me.

After a few days of me visiting our daughters, Sherry and I had a counseling session. Sherry was full of anger toward me. The counselor asked Sherry how she felt after I had done something kind for her the night before. Sherry acknowledged my action, but moved on to all the years of pain I had caused her. It would have been so easy to lash back at her, defensive over her anger at me despite treating her kindly. Fortunately, I remembered what my friend had said. I realized that I truly needed to listen to Sherry's words.

As I watched Sherry's facial expressions and body language, I knew that I was dealing with a very angry woman who needed to tell me how she felt. It took several years of letting Sherry tell me her pain to bring true healing to our relationship. Whenever I listened to her, which validated her feelings rather than arguing against them, it brought another measure of healing to her soul. I have learned that being truly sorry for the pain I have caused someone means being willing to listen to their expression of pain in equal measure to the time spent hurting them. To this day, I listen to Sherry when I have hurt her.

It would be so easy to diminish Sherry's words by looking at the situation from my perspective and wondering why she was upset. But that won't bring healing because it ignores her perspective. I've mentioned before that Sherry's love language is words of affirmation. My love language is attention. If Sherry teases me, it makes me feel loved because I like the attention. Teasing does not hurt my feelings. If I tease Sherry, knowing that words of affirmation are her love language, then I am possibly making her feel put down. It does not matter that teasing me makes me feel good. Teasing Sherry can make her feel bad. I have to ignore how I feel about teasing and give attention to how Sherry feels. If I blow off her perspective, by telling her that there is nothing wrong with my teasing or that she needs to grow up, all I have done is wound her heart further by not listening to her.

It took me years to learn to listen to other people's perspectives because I kept thinking the only perspective that was true was my own. Perspectives of reality are, in some ways, neither true nor untrue. They are only how we look at something or feel about it. Telling Sherry that her perspective of an event is not accurate is the same as saying her mind or emotions are faulty. No relationship will do well in those circumstances.

Imagine our car is rear-ended. No one is injured and there is no damage to the vehicles. Everything is fine in my view. I get back in the car and there are tears in Sherry's eyes. "What is wrong sweetheart?"

"That scared me," she says.

"Sherry, we were fortunate. No one was hurt and the vehicles are not damaged. Why are you upset?"

She then reminds me that when she was single, she was rear ended at fifty miles per hour. She still has problems with her neck to this day. Now I understand how a little bump can upset her. Our perspectives are different, but neither one is true or false. Both are accurate according to our individual experience of the event. What is important for me to understand is why Sherry feels the way she does. I have never been in a serious car accident so a minor accident means little to me. On the other hand, Sherry's response is understandable and valid. I can let her know her feelings are valid by listening to her.

When Sherry has a perspective that is different from mine, I need to understand why she feels that way rather than argue against it. For example, if she confronts me over hurting her feelings, telling her that I did not mean to hurt her does very little good. All I have done was put the focus on me. A more accurate response would be to say that I hear how she feels and apologize. In this way I keep the focus on her, validate her perspective, and give value to her as a person.

In our town is a church that, until recently, did not take its members to doctors or hospitals when they were sick or injured. They simply prayed for one another. Over the past few years three little babies at that church died because they were not given medical care. The state government decided to act and passed a law against using religion as a basis to deny medical care to children. When visiting Sherry, I told her that a husband and wife had just been sentenced to six years in prison for letting their baby die.

"Good!" Sherry responded with anger in her voice. I was surprised by her harshness toward the couple. I wanted to argue that families need to have the right to practice their religion without government interference. However, learning to listen was on my mind. So I asked why she felt that way. She explained: "Adults have the right to refuse medical care and are able to make an informed choice. Children cannot make an informed decision nor are they given a choice. It was the parents that refused care for their baby, and children should not have to die because of their parents' religious beliefs."

Because I listened, without thinking how to defend my opinion, I understand Sherry's perspective and I now agree with her on this issue. Listening to Sherry so I can understand her brought great healing to our relationship.

I learned to sense a person's spirit by looking for their facial expressions, especially their eyes. You can tell so much about how a woman feels if you notice her eyes. They reveal truth.

In an earlier chapter I mentioned the female manager at my paint store being put down by a client. I looked at her eyes and just for a moment they showed her discomfort. However, she quickly put on a smile and proceeded to follow his demand. The client never noticed the look in her eyes. He missed how he made her feel.

I have been around couples in which the husband publicly praises his wife. You can tell if his affirmation is accurate by looking at his wife's face. If she looks away from him as he speaks, then you know he is not telling the truth. Her refusal to look at him proves there are issues in the marriage.

Nowadays, I sometimes sense what Sherry wants or needs more by her facial expressions than her words. For instance, I tell her that I need to run to the store and she will start to say something but stop. I see that just for a moment she looked at the kitchen.

I look at the kitchen. The kitchen garbage can is full and the recycling bin is overflowing. She is buried in laundry. She did not ask me to help, but I can tell she wants the kitchen cleaned up before I leave. So, I turn and take out the garbage and recycling before I go.

Paying attention to Sherry makes her feel loved—and that is my goal.

11

I never consistently treated others with maturity and perfection.
How in the world can I demand they treat me perfectly?

The guy was screaming into his phone. Across the street I heard him angrily yell, "You are not taking my son away from me!" I assumed it was the mother on the other end of the line. Normally I would consider him a "nut case." But this time was different. I could see he was in fear—fear of losing his son. That fear drove him to anger—angry enough to vent his rage on a public sidewalk. I felt compassion for him.

This was not always the case. I have been a judgmental person. I have been quick to point out others' wrong behaviors and completely miss that I do similar actions. I expected to be forgiven for my failings but, in particular, expected Sherry to never do anything that wronged me. I was completely blind to how much I hurt her.

Often I angrily complained to Sherry about being late for a dinner party or activity. In my mind, she was making me look bad to others. She was embarrassing me. Never once did I ever consider how embarrassed I made her feel in front of her family. I confronted her in their presence and complained about how their visits disrupted my life. All I could see was my discomfort. I never thought of how unpleasant I made life for her. This hypocrisy in my life extended to others.

When Ellie and Nikki were little girls I taught them and their two friends how to shoot a BB gun. As I walked back from the target, I looked up. Nikki was pointing the loaded gun at me. I exploded in anger. I yelled at her to drop the gun and then berated her. I embarrassed her in front of her sister and friends. The real problem was not that I might have been shot in the eye, but that I had not told Nikki or the others about gun safety. I had never told her not to point a gun at someone. So, I should have firmly told her to put the gun down, and then apologized for not teaching her gun safety.

On another occasion we were camping. Ellie was sitting on the edge of a trailer. She lost her balance and fell onto our cooking table. Two legs broke off the table. I was furious. How would we cook our meals? The next minutes were spent berating her and stamping around the campsite expressing my anger. Not once did I consider that this was an accident. I was just mad that she had broken our table. Furthermore, I had no concern over whether she had hurt herself. The irony is that I had deliberately punched a hole in my parents' ceiling as an adult. Somehow I could overlook that fact, but couldn't extend grace to my daughter when her actions were not intentional, let alone wrong.

Since then I have tried to understand why I was so harsh on others' behaviors yet ignored my own wrongs. A number of reasons came to me. I realized that speaking negatively of others made me feel good about myself. I did not like my self-image, so putting others down made me feel better. One day I was riding with a friend of mine. I brought up the subject of someone who had cheated on their wife. My friend felt we should not discuss it. I was irritated. I wanted to talk about this other man's failings. It gave me pleasure to talk about other peoples' wrongs. If my friend would have joined in my discussion, then that sort of agreement would have provided a sense of unity between us. We were joined in mocking another person. We were better than that man.

Judging other people made me feel okay with being angry at them, particularly Sherry. Her mistakes justified my anger toward her. Early in our marriage, and before mobile phones were common, Sherry and her family attended an event out of town. I stayed home with Ellie. As the evening wore into night I began to worry. I called the highway patrol to see if there had been an accident. There had not. What had occurred, as it became so late, was Sherry did not call because she believed I had gone to bed. When her sister and brother-in-law arrived home with her, I could barely speak to them. I was furious at her for making me worry. In my mind, I was justified in being angry at her for her failure to call me.

Finally, I believed in a cause and effect view of the world. This led me to believe that people suffered the consequences of their actions. In other words, they got what they deserved. I knew a family whose daughter was dating an abusive young man. Both her family and others warned her. She ignored their caution, married him, and they had a child. Within a year, the husband beat the baby to death. Sherry and I were both aware of her family's warnings. After we heard of the child's death, Sherry's reaction was one of great sorrow for the mother. I believed none of this would have ever happened if the mother had listened to her family. Sherry's thinking was compassionate. My thoughts were judgmental.

What changed me from judgmental to compassionate? Please understand that this was not an easy process. Overcoming a poor self-image by looking down on others is not easy to transform. To this day I have to observe my thoughts and how I think of other people. It is now easier to think of myself as not better than and not less than others, but I still have to guard against those lies. If I see myself looking down on others, then I know there is something missing in my life, and I am trying to compensate for it by judging others.

Perhaps the most significant impact causing me to be compassionate was acknowledging that I had committed great wrongs. I was not a great person who lost his temper. I was a man who destroyed his family. I was not a man with a little issue of anger. I was someone who at times acted like a monster.

In my recovery group were men whose anger led to committing crimes against women. For the longest time I believed I was better than them. But when I saw that I had done horrible evil against my family, I knew I was no different. I was an evil-behaving man. I definitely was not some perfect person.

This was extremely hard to accept. The guilt and shame were painful. I wanted to believe that I was not a man who committed evil deeds. I did not want to consider that my anger was so damaging. It was painful to consider how wrong I was. But acknowledging the evil softened my attitude toward others. I was not better than them. Instead, I was one of them. Trying to believe that I was better than others, in spite of my failings, was a lie. I believed this lie because it made me feel good about myself in spite of the wrongs I committed.

I was torn between ignoring what I had done so I could feel good about myself, and admitting my evil so I could proceed ahead in recovery. Consider a person who keeps denying they have an infection in their leg. In spite of the pain, they ignore help because they are fearful of doctors scraping open the infection and applying medicine, which could cause increased pain (initially). The outcome, though, will be a chance at life. Ignoring the infection will ultimately lead to death.

For years Sherry asked me to get help. I talked to a few men and each one of them told me how angry they got. Many encouraged me to not be so hard on myself. They offered no help at all. The one woman I spoke with, looked me in the eye, and told me to take my anger problem seriously. I ignored her. I never sought counseling or professional help. I felt guilt for my anger, but did not want to take the initial painful steps of seeking recovery.

When Sherry left, I could have continued to ignore my problems and become even more enraged at her. But instead, the horrible consequences of my anger infection were so great that I entered into recovery and started professional counseling to receive the help I needed.

As part of that recovery process, I had to face the evil I had done. It was terrible to realize how horrible of a person I was. The shame was immense. The guilt was overwhelming. But this was the consequence of seeing me for who I am. This was tearing back the skin in order to allow the infection to come out. This honest realization gave me compassion for other men who are angry.

In turn, that compassion is at the heart of writing this book. I'm no better than anyone else. My honest confessions on these pages have made that abundantly clear. Yet...

God loved me and forgave me.

O God, O God, O God! It is all so horrible and nightmarish what I have done. The horror of my sin. Why didn't I let God work in my life thirty years ago? My family is paying the price for my fear of trusting God. I have been so fearful and stubborn. So afraid to trust God. Forgive me, Lord. I am so sorry. (journal entry)

The best answer I had for my poor self-image, shame, and guilt, was to cry out to God to forgive me and transform my character. This was not easy. At times I had great fear that God could not change me. I was lost in a pit of fear, anger, control, selfishness, and now shame and guilt. I was fearful that I was so damaged inside that I could not be changed into a loving person.

I can't love Sherry if I am afraid, for the fear will control me and turn my actions into fighting the fear rather than loving Sherry, regardless of what she chooses to do. But without fear I am able to love her rather than trying to care of myself. (journal entry)

O God, please help me love! Please help me put others first. Please help me feel for others rather than myself. (journal entry)

There were times when I came to realize that God had forgiven me and that he was working to change my life. There were other times when I doubted I could be changed. Back and forth it went. Finally, there came a day when I knew inside that I was forgiven and that God was working in my life. This assurance made me feel loved and caused me not to lift myself above others. I did not need to increase my self-image. I was loved by my Creator.

This does not mean that I was automatically forgiven by my wife, my daughters, or all the other people who were so wounded by me. I did not know if my wife would ever love me again. In fact, I did not deserve for her to love me. I deserved to be divorced, have my possessions taken, and be given limited access to our daughters. That is what I deserved.

But I was granted mercy by God and by others. I did nothing to deserve it. Yet I received the love of God and others. A number of friends of Sherry and mine did something wonderful for me. They did not condone what I had done and they did not condemn me. They knew I was an angry man, but they still loved me.

The love of God and his forgiveness of my evil, as I admitted and turned from it, took away my guilt and shame. I regret how I have lived, but I no longer feel guilt or shame for it. This was different than in the past. In the past, I would apologize to Sherry and the girls for my angry outbursts. I would ask God to forgive me, but I did not change. I just kept blowing up in anger over and over again. Nothing changed. As Sherry would say, "Stop saying you are sorry. Your apologies mean nothing. Change your actions!"

In recovery, I not only asked God to forgive me, but I also began to change my behaviors. After two years in recovery, I wrote letters of apology to Sherry, the girls, my parents, and others. I described how I must have made them feel and told them how sorry I was for hurting them. I never asked for their forgiveness. Reestablishing a relationship with me was not something I was trying to achieve in my apologies. I simply wanted to bring healing to them.

What brought forgiveness between my family and me was not apologizing and admitting my wrongs, as helpful as that was to them. Rather, it was the change in my behaviors. That was what they were looking for. I was able to do this because I had the forgiveness and love of God. His forgiveness and love took away my shame and guilt. No longer was I focused on the negative emotions within me. I was loved! I could now turn my attention away from myself and onto others. Losing shame and guilt freed me from a negative self-image. I didn't need to elevate myself above others.

I came to understand why I was so angry. I understood my motivations. This helped me to understand why other people were so angry, as well. Seeing that my anger came from fear, I was able to look beyond other people's anger and see the fear in them.

In my painting work, I will often encounter clients who are extremely difficult. Some are perfectionists; others scrutinize every step of the process, pointing out what hasn't been completed. As painful as their demands, rude behaviors, and expectations are, I can see they are frightened that I might do poor quality work or defraud them. If I want to have an easier time with them, I realize I need to alleviate their fears so they can trust me. Fear of pain is what motivated my anger. I need to see the fear in others instead of merely their anger.

I was painting a lady's house. All we had left to paint was her handrail system and the front door. Because the temperature was so hot she wanted us to wait until a day when it was cooler. I agreed and told her we would return the next week. The next week we were so busy with other jobs that we were not able to return. Over that weekend I received a letter telling me she was filing a complaint against me with the state regulatory agency. I called. She did not return my call. I could not understand why she was upset.

Eventually, two employees from my paint supplier, who knew her, visited her and told her she should let me finish the work. She agreed. On getting to her home, I could have been angry at her for the trouble she caused me. Instead, I asked her if she had thought I was not going to return to do the work. She agreed that is why she intended to file a complaint. Fear of being defrauded led to her actions. Fortunately, understanding her fear led me to finish the job without being angry at her.

Being in recovery has helped me become more compassionate to others. Sometimes people have problems with how I drive. As a child I enjoyed watching the TV cartoon character, Mr. Magoo. He was an elderly man who was very near-sighted. He drove down sidewalks, hit fire hydrants, and in general created great mayhem for everyone around him. I drive a bit like Mr. Magoo.

Other drivers honk at me. They are not smiling when they do. Sometimes they yell profane comments out their windows in my direction and make obscene hand gestures. It bothers me how poorly I drive, but there is one good point in the whole experience. I don't get mad at other people for their reaction to my driving. I do not like their anger, but I understand it. I have spent enough time in recovery that I know why they respond the way they do. They feel powerless around me. They are afraid I might hit them. If I turn in front of them, they feel disrespected. I understand their thinking.

I discovered that judging others was not love. When I realized I am loved by God, even during the worst behaviors of my life, it led me to love others in their difficult moments. One of my employees began showing up late for work. Additionally, he would not call me. Suffice it to say, it was frustrating. After the last occurrence, in which I found out there was a family emergency, I told him we would talk the next work day.

The first words he spoke to me when we met were to apologize and tell me he did not understand why I had not fired him yet. I looked him in the eye.

"You are more important to me than just as an employee. You are a person I care about." I asked him what was happening with his family and their situation. When we finished talking, he promised to notify me in the future if there was a problem with showing up on time for work.

A few weeks after this conversation I met with my paint representative. He had talked to my employee and told me that the employee loved working for me. I mentioned that it was surprising to me, but he seemed to enjoy painting.

"No," said the paint representative. "He loves working for you."

His missing work caused me difficulties, but I still had compassion for this man. He was far more important to me than the damage his tardiness caused me. That compassion influenced him positively. He is not tardy anymore and if he needs to miss work, he calls me the day before.

When I was in the midst of my rage, my family still reached out to me in love. They hated what I did but they loved me. As my counselor use to say in group therapy, "There is something good in you men or your wives or girlfriends would have never put up with the way you treated them. They loved you."

If God and my family could love me in the midst of my anger, I have no reason not to reach out in love to others in their worst moments.

I caused the effects in my life. Sherry left me because of how I treated her and our daughters. I still believe in a cause and effect world. However, because I realized what I brought onto my family, I cannot judge someone else for the pain they bring on themselves. For so long in my life I looked down on others who destroyed their marriages because of an affair. I saw "evil" all over them. Finally, I began to see "evil" all over me. The can of red paint I sprayed on others, by my criticisms, was now running off of me. My own feet were standing in a red puddle.

Furthermore, I can see only the obvious causes of certain effects. I do not know all the hidden causes that go into an effect. Chaos Theory suggests that a butterfly flapping its wings in Brazil eventually causes a tornado in Texas. In other words, we cannot see all the influences that impact effects. I do not know every person's history, motivations, or pains. They will pay the consequences for their wrongs, but I feel for their pain.

The terrible deeds I did to my family, and the mercy I received, have taken away my desire to look down on others. I have never consistently treated others with maturity and perfection. So, how can I demand they treat me perfectly?

12

Religion and politics are two topics that should not be discussed if I want to avoid a potential argument. Sherry has also asked that I not talk about sex. If you were hoping for a tidbit of information about how moving away from anger affected our sex lives...sorry. It will not happen. I wanted to include it, but my much wiser wife finds it intrusive and unnecessary. Again, I apologize. There is one topic I do want to discuss and that is religion. There is a very good reason to include the subject in this book. Have you ever met an angry religious person? Their demeanor is contrary to the effect one would assume a relationship with God should produce. Angry religious people seem doubly wrong, I think.

In the acclaimed 1977 television series, *Roots,* a slave walks into his master's study without permission. The slave owner erupts in anger, shouting at the slave to leave and never interrupt him again. He then returns to reading his Bible. This was an angry religious man.

Prior to owning a painting company, I was in the ministry for almost thirty years. I taught people how to love others, forgive, and get over anger. I considered myself an example of goodness. I was disciplined in prayer and Bible study. I was also angry, unloving, and dominating of my family. Anyone who has read even a little of the Bible will know that my life was in direct conflict with biblical teaching. I was a dreaded angry religious man.

I grew up in a church that emphasized devotion to God. Historically, how they expressed it was by adherence to outward behaviors. They wanted to be godly in their actions so they rejected a number of behaviors that were common in the world. They did not drink alcohol, smoke, take drugs (not even caffeine). They did not attend theater shows and when movies arrived they avoided them, as well. They argued against dancing and listening to popular music. They paid great attention to the clothes they wore believing that clothing could make one vain. They wore simple clothes and rejected any jewelry, including wedding rings.

My great grandfather was a leader in the early days of the church. To him, devotion to God meant neglecting neckties, as this was a form of vanity for a man. This controversy became so difficult within the church that he eventually left to join another church with similar beliefs. I will say, in his defense, that later in life he is reported as saying, "What does wearing or not wearing a necktie have to do with holiness?"

This emphasis on one's outward performance for God was the spirit of the church I grew up in. Growing up I did not attend movies, go to dances, drink alcohol, gamble, smoke, or play cards. While my family emphasized love for others, what I really remember was that devotion to God meant not doing those forbidden activities. This led me to believe that anyone who does those things was not as devoted to God as I was. While encouraged within my home to have a loving relationship with God, my view of God was all about following outward rules.

I wanted to be perfect in my behavior so God would be pleased with me. For me outward behaviors were what were important to God. Christianity seemed to be about what I did *not* do. There was safety in this system. Follow the rules and you are safe. God is pleased with you. Of course, very little emphasis was put on the inward quality of my life. So pride, anger, lust, and jealousy existed in me, but they were not as important. Following the church standards was most significant.

This made me judgmental of others and unloving in my heart toward them. I particularly looked down on Sherry if she had different standards than me. I felt morally superior to her for my beliefs. Somehow I missed that I was terrible at loving others and that she was wonderful at loving others. I still felt better than her because I believed I had great religious standards of right and wrong.

Because following the rules was proof of devotion to God, I wanted Sherry to believe and live exactly like me in her relationship with God.

Because she did not, I worried that she was not devoted like me. I needed to be responsible for her relationship with God.

One day we were at church. I noticed that Sherry's blouse had slipped down, exposing a bit of cleavage and so I told her, in front of another person, because I was embarrassed. My lack of love shamed her, but at least I was upholding my moral standards. I could not see how unloving I was to her.

Over the years I looked down on any person whose convictions were different from mine. The only way I could feel close to another person was if they had the same beliefs I did. If they did not, then I was better than them. I was trying to convince myself that I was perfect for God. God has to like me since I am doing what he likes and others are not.

It was only later that I realized that my belief is one of the founding principles behind religious fanaticism. In other words, if your behavior is wrong toward God, and my behavior is what God desires, then I can treat you as I wish on God's behalf. It does not matter whether I am a Christian, Jewish, or Muslim. I can treat others horribly because they are not in God's will.

This religious superiority toward others shows in my journal writing prior to recovery: *Lately it seems that so many professing Christian couples are ending their marriages and so many professing Christians are drinking. I just don't understand it in terms of obeying God. Apparently, they just don't care what God thinks.*

I remember a time when I was leading a Bible study for a group of college students. One of the students mentioned reading *Playboy* magazine. I asked how he could uphold that behavior while being a Christian. He did not see a problem with it. My perspective was, not only was his behavior wrong, but also he was not a good person. I was a better person in God's eyes than him. I was morally superior.

I had the same idea of moral superiority toward Sherry. When we were first married, I discovered that she does not pray to God in the same manner as I do. In my mind, one must get up early and pray for a long time; the longer, the better. This is the correct manner in which to pray. Sherry needs more sleep than I do. She does not get up early and pray. When we pray together she often prays shorter prayers than I do. I saw her as spiritually weak with God. By praying in the "correct manner," I am pleasing God and therefore spiritually better than my wife.

Sherry often felt the pressure of my religiously superior attitude toward her. What I now see is that I ignored God speaking to me about my behavior toward my family. Sherry, on the other hand, cried out to God and heard him tell her what to do. God heard her prayers. I wanted Sherry to change. God ignored my prayers and changed me.

During recovery, I was reading a passage from the Bible. This was a story Jesus told about a Pharisee, one of the Jewish religious leaders from that time, and a tax-gatherer, who was hated by the Jewish people because they collected taxes for the occupying Roman government.

> [Jesus] told this parable to certain ones who trusted in themselves that they were righteous, and viewed others with contempt: Two men went up into the temple to pray. One a Pharisee, and the other a tax-gatherer. The Pharisee stood and was praying thus to himself, "God, I thank thee that I am not like other people: swindlers, unjust, adulterers, or even like this tax-gatherer. I fast twice a week; I pay tithes of all that I get."

> But the tax-gatherer, standing some distance away, was even unwilling to lift up his eyes to heaven, but was beating his breast, saying, "God, be merciful to me, the sinner!" I tell you, this man went down to his house justified rather than the other; for everyone who exalts himself shall be humbled, but he who humbles himself shall be exalted.

I was a hypocrite. The worst abuse a person can level at a church minister is that they are a phony, a hypocrite. I saw it. I was a fake. In the previous chapter, I mentioned a young woman who ignored the warnings she received about her abusive boyfriend. After they got married, and had their first child, he beat that infant to death. I was religiously correct that she should have obeyed the warnings that God gave her, but I had no compassion for her.

> *[Jesus said,] Woe to you Pharisees! For you pay tithe of mint and rue and every garden herb, and disregard justice and the love of God; but these are the things you should have done without neglecting the others.*

Jesus continues to speak and addresses my terrible view of Christianity as looking good outwardly but inwardly being full of wicked beliefs and attitudes. I saw myself in his words.

> *Woe to you, scribes and Pharisees, hypocrites! For you are like whitewashed tombs which on the outside appear beautiful, but inside they are full of dead men's bones and all uncleanness. Even so you too outwardly appear righteous to men, but inwardly you are full of hypocrisy and lawlessness.*

To change my religious beliefs, I needed to view Christianity in an accurate way. Sherry was the person who helped show me how. In the healing program she attended, she heard: *God is both Love and The Law. The Law is always there to support his Love. Anytime the Law is elevated above is Love, it is always abusive.*

I had focused on obeying God's outward laws by prayer, church attendance, and Bible study. I missed out badly on loving people. In the past I would be upset if Sherry missed church because she was tired. Little did I care for how she felt, only that she follow what I saw as religious law. I put the law above love, every time.

My eyes began to open when I saw that God had already given me a description of what it means to be inwardly mature.

> *The fruit of the Spirit is love, joy, peace, patience, kindness, goodness, faithfulness, gentleness, self-control.*

I saw these character traits are the outcome of allowing God's Spirit to work freely within my life. They are the Spirit of God, not moral standards. If you squeeze a grape, then grape juice comes out. If you squeeze a godly person, then the attributes of God are exhibited. When life's circumstances squeezed me, what came out were anger, irritation, and fear. It did not matter that I tried to look religious on the outside. What was in me came out of me under stress.

I came to realize that I trusted in my convictions rather than God's love for me. I believed my convictions were what kept me right with God. If I disobeyed, then I was sinning. I needed to radically change my view of relating with God. God was not pleased by my obedience to rules any more than he was with the religious leaders of Jesus' time. I needed to learn what his heart longed for in me. His desire was for compassion, love, kindness, and mercy. These were the issues that mattered to him. My pastor told me, "Brent, you have personal convictions of what is right and wrong, but you do not have love for others."

"Should I throw away my convictions?" I asked.

"No. But you need to have love for others and not convictions alone."

It was time to move from following rules to a healthy and proper relationship with God and others.

Sherry told me that I was religiously hard, but after I went through recovery we both noticed that I had become softer in my beliefs. I still have convictions, but they are not what I trust for a relationship with God. I still follow my personal convictions because I believe God told them to me. (Can you imagine an angry man drinking? Being an angry drunk is not God's will for me!) But love is more important than my convictions. I came to realize that devotion to God primarily meant loving others with God's kind of love. God's love is always more important than my convictions.

Shortly before Sherry and the girls moved away, we held a weekly Bible study in our home. One of the members was Sherry's boss. We decided that each week a different member of the group would lead the Bible study. Sherry's boss asked to lead a study. The problem for me was that she belonged to a religious group that wasn't close enough to orthodox Christian beliefs. Sherry believed that this woman had a tremendous heart for knowing God in spite of her belief system. I could not see how Sherry thought this woman knew God since her beliefs were so far apart from ours.

After my recovery program I became acquainted with a business owner. He was a member of the same church as Sherry's boss. As we talked, I realized that he had more integrity than any business owner I knew. He had clients who refused to pay him the amount of money they agreed to. He finished the job for them anyway. His ethics were outstanding. He seemed to have a genuine heart for God.

I know that for many Christians, not believing all of the orthodox Christian teachings about Jesus means you are wrong about God. But Sherry and I see these two people as genuine seekers after God. They do not believe what we think are accurate teachings, but we sense their desire to know God according to the knowledge they possess. I have come to the conclusion that God is the judge of their heart, not me. I am not more devoted to God than they are. I am only responsible for how I respond to God's voice in my own life.

For years I believed that keeping outward convictions was the way to please God. I was proud and judgmental toward those who did not follow my convictions. I was wrong. God was far more interested if I had mercy, compassion, and love for others. To paraphrase an old saying: *Religion is man's attempt to be right with God. Instead, relationship with God, and love for others, makes us right with him.*

I said I loved God, but was hard on people. That was dead wrong. Loving God means loving people. I believe this is the true heart of God.

13

I believed so many lies in my life. These lies brought great destruction to my family and me. In this book, *Confessions of an Angry Man,* I have written about eleven belief changes that needed to occur in order for my outward behaviors to be transformed.

Here is what I came to believe, and still believe with all my heart.

1. I was wrong and needed to change. Prior, Sherry was the problem. If she would just do what I wanted, then I would be happy. I was unable to see that I was self-centered. One of the greatest gifts I have ever been given was having my eyes opened after Sherry left me. In that horribly painful moment, I realized I was the problem in the marriage, and not her. It was the beginning of walking out of darkness and into the light.

2. Anger was not an addiction. Throughout my life I believed that anger was something I could not control. I could not help myself when I exploded. The truth was that anger happened very fast in me but, if I could slow down and change my thinking, I could develop new behaviors to painful events. The process of slowing and changing my thinking—a technique the recovery program taught me—enabled me to think outside of the emotions of pain and anger. I could react to the pain in a healthy way that did not destroy others' emotions or my own.

3. God loved me. Recently, Sherry and I were at a fundraiser. We heard the stories of angry people as well as the testimony of a woman who had suffered greatly from an angry partner. All three of them had participated in the recovery program I had gone through. In all of their accounts, the central reality that changed their lives was realizing that God loved them. Affirming that God loved me took me away from looking after my needs to focusing on loving others.

4. Listen to my wife. There is no one in the world who loves me as much as Sherry. There is also no one else that knows me better than her. She sees all the character flaws in me that I cannot see. I did not want to hear her correction. It still is not fun, but it is life-giving. She helps me become more successful as a husband, father, employer, son, and friend. If God can speak through a donkey to a wayward prophet, surely he can speak needed words of correction through Sherry. I just have to be sure to listen.

5. The true meaning of leadership. God's view of leadership is completely upside down to society's view. In our culture, leadership means to boss people around; to take authority and use your power, including anger, to get what you want. God's view is that you do not command others, but rather influence them by your example. Being of service to others is the heart of leadership. I suspect that former President Jimmy Carter has done more for this country serving with Habitat for Humanity than he did as president. For decades, he has led by his example of service. I want my wife and daughters to follow the good in my life, not because I command it, but because they are influenced by my example of service.

6. Angry control is never acceptable. There are thousands of reasons to angrily control others, but no valid reason. Anger against someone who offends me never brings good. I once got in a disagreement over the amount a client owed. It was in the thousands of dollars. We eventually sat down and we agreed on a much lower price. Our emotions were raw over the problem and it could have ended quite badly. Instead, I asked for a favor. He looked at me with some surprise.

"Will you mentor me?" I asked. He was a wealthy businessman who knew more than I did about how to run a business. He was quiet for a while.

"Will you do what I say?" he eventually asked.

"Yes."

I could have turned him into an enemy of mine after losing $7,000. Instead, I turned him into a potential friend and mentor. I should add, later he gave me much more work on another property. Abraham Lincoln is quoted as saying, "Do I not destroy my enemies when I make them my friends?" No matter how I am treated, I do not want to take out anger on them. It only brings heartache.

7. Trust God to meet my needs. No one else, especially Sherry, is responsible for making me happy. My goal in life is not to use my family to serve my needs. My goal is to depend on God to take care of me. If I am lonely or sad, I go to God to hear from him.

8. Willingness to go through suffering. I do not like emotional pain. But if I medicate the pain, then I will never learn what is causing it. If I have an infection in my body and all I do is take pain pills, but never go to the doctor to learn what causes the infection, I will eventually die. If all I do with emotional pain is medicate it with drugs, alcohol, anger, sex addiction, gambling, or any of a host of other coping mechanisms, then what is causing that pain is never healed and will destroy me. I want to be healed of the pain I am angry about, and I need to live through it, and experience God's healing rather than medicate and ignore it.

9. Listen and validate others' perspectives. Hearing the hurt I caused Sherry was difficult. It would have been easy in the moment to explain that I did not mean to hurt her or that she misunderstood my motives. That perspective would have made me feel better, but it would not have helped Sherry. Whether or not I meant to hurt her is not the point. The point is to listen to her and validate how I made her feel. In so doing it brings healing to her and eventually healing to me. Denial is a great name for an Egyptian river, but it is a horrible reaction to another person's pain.

10. Accept others' failings. Honestly accepting the guilt of my wrong helped me be more sympathetic to the failings of others. I now can understand their behaviors. It does not decrease the hurt they cause me, but it gives me understanding and helps me to have compassion for them. Years ago I felt betrayed by a friend. I carried the hurt of that offense for fifteen years. He never apologized and I struggled to forgive him until one particular day. I was thinking about him and how he never admitted his wrong. I began to wonder if there were people who had been hurt by me and I didn't even know it. I had never apologized to them because I was unaware I had done wrong. It came to me that perhaps this is what happened to my friend. He never apologized because he never knew how he hurt me. In that moment I was able to forgive him because I understood him. To be forgiving brings healing. Anger brings only more pain.

11. Replace religion with love. Obeying my religious convictions does not make me right with God. They also do not make me better than others. They only make me proud. For years I felt like a failure to God because of my anger, lust, jealousy, and lack of love. So I tried to improve my standing with God by obeying all of my outward convictions of right and wrong behaviors. They only made me a hypocrite. Admitting that I was wrong in my life brought trust, transformation, and love for others. Loving my family became my new goal.

Many other old beliefs of mine also needed to change so I could live without fear and in love with my family. You'll find the lists of these "Old Beliefs" and "New Beliefs" on pages 130 and 131.

What has been most helpful to reduce the risk of returning to angry and controlling behaviors?
1. Rejecting the lie that for life to be good, I have to get my way or circumstances need to go my way. This is the thinking of a child and I want to live as an adult.
2. Recognize that for me, selfishness and self-centeredness are core beliefs that "justify" angry and controlling actions.
3. Reject the notion that for life to be safe, I have to control people and circumstances.

I now believe that I do not have to get my way, nor should I, for life to be good. Additionally, rejecting selfishness and instead serving others, especially my wife and children, is a primary means of defeating selfishness and power and control behaviors. I consciously try not to control Sherry, nor question or argue with her about her beliefs or behaviors. Learning to trust God and recognize that he truly has my best interests at heart, helps me not to worry and not try to control circumstances and people. As well, I have come to believe that my wife's feelings, our children's feelings, as well as every other person's feelings, are more important to me than getting my way.

For quite a long time during my recovery, I started my day by making a statement and asking a question. The statement was, "I am not in control. I do not want to be in control. Lord, you are in control of my life." The question was, "Lord, what do you want me to do today?" Often, what I sensed was to trust him. I also remind myself often that I do not have to get my way for life to be good.

There are several warning signs I recognize prior to relapsing. Being extremely tired or focusing narrowly on one issue and avoiding others' needs. I do this often when we are packing to leave on vacation. All I can think of is getting packed and leaving on time. I do not pay attention to how irritable or frustrated I am and how it makes my family feel. All that matters is that we go, now! This is called tunnel vision and I need to change.

Feeling pressured and stressed, irritable, raising my voice, muttering to myself, having an annoyed expression, or preaching at our girls, are additional warning signs. Feeling anxious and repeating myself is another. So is thinking negative thoughts about myself or others. Finally, when I begin to complain about or curse my circumstances.

Recently, Sherry and I attended a fundraising banquet for the recovery program I joined. We waited and waited in line to get into the parking lot. Looking up ahead, I saw that the hotel had installed a toll gate. Slowly, one car after another would creep through because a guard had to input an entrance card for each car.

I began to complain, over and over, to Sherry, how ridiculous it was to allow only one car in at a time. I thought they should have just lifted the gate and let everyone in at once. Finally, I recognized what I was doing. It took some effort, but I finally stopped complaining and avoided becoming angry.

Old Beliefs

1. Sherry is out to hurt me

2. I have to control Sherry so she doesn't hurt me

3. I have to change our children

4. It is my family's job to make me happy

5. I have a right to be abusively angry with my family

6. My family should be gracious to me when I am angry

7. My needs are most important

8. I have to control life so I can be safe

9. I have to look out for myself as no one else will

10. It is okay to touch Sherry's body whenever

11. I have to be in charge since I am the man

12. When we disagree, my beliefs are right and Sherry's are wrong

13. I have to win arguments

14. God's character is obeying man-made standards

15. I can let my mind think whatever I want

16. I should have my way in what happens with our possessions, finances, and the children

17. It is important that Sherry understand me

18. Keeping myself comfortable is most important

19. Sherry should not present problems to me, but solve them herself

20. Sherry is attacking me

21. I know more than Sherry and I have to keep my own counsel and ignore hers

New Beliefs

1. Sherry wants the best for our family

2. Controlling Sherry hurts her. I trust God

3. I need to be an example to the girls

4. It is my responsibility to care for myself

5. I have no such right. "There are a million reasons and no excuses to be abusively angry." It is wrong.

6. I should be gracious to my family

7. Others' needs are most important

8. I need to trust God to be safe

9. God keeps me safe as I trust him

10. I touch with her permission

11. God made Sherry and me equal marriage partners

12. My beliefs are not naturally right. I can be wrong. Sherry can be correct

13. It is better to listen and validate

14. God's character is the fruit of the Holy Spirit

15. I bring my thoughts to God's approval

16. Sherry and I are partners and I defer to her opinion and desires and partner with her in decisions

17. It is important that I hear and understand Sherry

18. Serving my family is more important than my comfort

19. I am Sherry's husband. I love her and it is my privilege to help her

20. Sherry is not my enemy. She is my ally

21. God speaks through Sherry to bless our family and to help me become more Christ-like

What I intend to do when I notice warning signs is to slow down physically and mentally. I take long deep breaths, which bring oxygen to the part of the brain where I think rationally. I pray, take breaks, maybe go for a walk, and ask why I am stressed or becoming angry. When I catch myself thinking negative thoughts, I replace them with positive thinking.

I try to stay emotionally calm when correcting my daughters. Instead of trying to secure my own comfort when they are upset or arguing with me, I seek to discover what is bothering them and try to comfort them. I now refuse to use discipline as punishment. Instead, I provide consequences for their bad decisions in order to get their attention and teach them new ways to deal with their situations. Taking the car away from my teenagers or removing mobile phones arrests their attention so they will calm down and listen. I do not use discipline as a way to take out my anger on them as in the past.

I do not try to change their minds or my wife's. I do not need to win arguments. If the girls, or Sherry, do not agree with my perspective, then I do not need to prove it to them. If I am right, then God can prove it to them. I do not need to lord it over them. What I do desire is to trust God as Lord over me.

I mentioned earlier in this book that Sherry told me that I base all my decisions on fear. When I realized that God loved me, and had the best for my family, then I no longer had to angrily control my family so we could remain safe.

In the animated film, *The Croods,* a prehistoric family is dominated by an angry and controlling husband and father, Grug. They live in a dark cave afraid of the wild animals that live outside. The only way he knows to help his family survive the dangers of caveman life is his belief, "Always be afraid and live in the dark."

When a stranger warns them of approaching danger, the family wants to leave the cave and find a new home, but Grug is fearful. The stranger and Grug's family warn him throughout the film, but he sticks to his old belief until he is forced by circumstances to change at the last minute. At the end of the film he proclaims his new belief, "Never be afraid and live in the light."

I was Grug: Always afraid and living in darkness so we could be safe. Eventually, I came to believe that, by trusting God, I could not be afraid and live in God's light. God is much better at dealing with my family than I am, with my limited abilities and wisdom.

I said I went through recovery. Let me correct that statement. I went through a recovery program for more than two years, but I am not finished. I am still in recovery for the rest of my life. I continue to learn from Sherry, my program, others, and the Lord how to live in love. My transformation is not complete, but it is much farther down the road than a few short years ago.

14

Rodger and I were safe on top of the pinnacle at Smith Rock. However, we could not see how to get down to level ground. As I mentioned earlier, our plan at the beginning of the climb was to walk off the top of the cliff and down a trail. That was not possible. We had mistakenly misjudged where we were at the bottom of the cliff. We weren't at the top of the cliff. We were at the top of a four-foot wide ridge with hundreds of feet to the river in front of us and hundreds of feet to the ground behind us. So, we still had the problem of getting down.

We climbed to the other side of the pinnacle. Jutting out from the face of the cliff was a tiny ledge with a four-foot tall pillar of rock at its edge. Rodger thought we could wrap a climbing sling around the pillar, tie two ropes together and thread them through the sling. We could then rappel down the cliff to a steep dirt slope, and then climb down to the river. There were a couple of problems with this. One, between us and the ledge was air. We could not walk or climb to the ledge. We had to jump to it. Two, were the ropes long enough to reach the ground? Or would we come to the end of the ropes and be left dangling on the side of the cliff, far from the ground below? Regardless, it was our one and only way off the pinnacle.

Rodger jumped first. As he landed, he grabbed the rock pillar instantly to prevent falling off the other side of the ledge. When I landed, he caught and stopped me. We carefully stood on this tiny ledge over a hundred feet in the air. We set up the rappel system and anxiously looked over the side as we lowered the ropes. Their ends just touched the ground. We were going to make it all the way. We rappelled down the cliff, grateful that we had survived the climb and had overcome both problems that could have ended badly.

Sherry and I have been together for more than three and a half years. After our breakup, we wondered if we would ever be together again. It has been a miracle of transformation and healing. However, we still face problems. My father died a year ago. Shortly after that I had a stroke. Both of our mothers are elderly and face long-term health requirements. We have two teenage daughters who need funding for college. Sherry and I have the same problems everyone else has. What is different is that we face them together. I no longer get angry at life's circumstances and therefore do not take out my frustration on her or our daughters. Additionally, I am still learning how to live as a partner with my wife.

Our youngest daughter, Nikki, plays volleyball and basketball. We know the parents and their kids as we have watched our children play sports together through the years. It is like a family. Recently I was loudly running verbal commentary about the volleyball game. People thought I was funny. One lady told me that she loved sitting near me because I made her laugh. I felt good. Sherry had a different perspective.

She told me that my comments were "over the top." In other words, I was somewhat shocking in what I said.

"But people were laughing. The one lady said I made her laugh."

"Yes, she and her husband were laughing, but it was a nervous laughter. They were surprised by your words."

There were several thoughts I had in one second flat. The first was that uneasy feeling inside that I was being corrected. Immediately came the thought to remain calm and listen. The next thought I had was to defend myself.

In my mind, a dialogue started—between me and myself.

"I like being funny. This is who I am. If I can't be funny, then I might as well just shut up and be silent. I cannot even be me."

"Why do you want people to laugh at you?"

"It makes me feel good. I like the attention."

"So you make people laugh to draw attention to yourself? Isn't that self-focused? Hasn't being self-focused been part of the problem in your life? Do you make people laugh to bless them, or do you do it to meet your own needs?"

"To tell the truth, I do not even think of other people. I do it to make myself feel good."

This dialogue continued in my mind for several days. Sherry's correction had caused me to think about why I talk to people. I thought I wanted to be the kind of person who makes others think they are the most important person in the world. How can I do that for others if my whole reason for talking is to bring attention to myself?

I realized that I needed to change the motivation for why I talk. I needed to learn to express attention to others. I needed to say words that encouraged them and made them feel good about themselves.

After several days, I thanked Sherry for talking with me and my need to guard my words at games. I told her about my internal dialogue. She looked at me and said, "You have no idea how you just made me feel. You really listened to me."

She was aware that I was preparing to speak to a group of men on the topic of listening to their wives. She was concerned that if I told men to listen to their wives, they would fear their wives would nag them.

"Brent, tell them that their wives will not nag them if they listen. When a woman feels listened to, then they know they do not have to repeat themselves. Their husbands have heard them."

Please do not think that our relationship is one-sided. As Sherry and I have healed, I am now able to speak in love to Sherry about situations with her. One night we were having dinner with her sister and brother-in-law. I began to tell them a story about one of Nikki's art projects.

"They already know that story," Sherry interrupted.

I stopped talking and felt that uneasy feeling of discomfort inside. *Stay calm and loving*, I told myself. The next day I brought up the subject to Sherry. Without anger or frustration, I told her that it felt that I was being told to shut up.

"Oh my word! You're exactly right. That's exactly what I did to you," she said. "What I was trying to do was save you from going through the whole story when they already had heard, but the way I did it came off very harsh."

I suggested that we come up with a way to express that idea without making a person feel like they have to shut up. Sherry thought of a better way to communicate in the future.

In that exchange, we walked through a communication problem where, in the past, I would have erupted in anger and frustration. Instead, we solved a problem as partners who are sensitive to each other. This is a type of intimacy we never had prior to my recovery.

Many times we have been surprised by the depth and honesty of our conversations as we have grown in our trust in each other. One night Sherry and I were driving home from one of Nikki's away games. As we drove through the night, down the beautiful Columbia Gorge, she told me about an encounter she had recently had with a former boyfriend who worked at the same job she did. He came into her office and spoke with her for a moment. She felt uncomfortable about the familiarity she felt. She had dated him for quite a long time and it was understandable that there would be feelings of familiarity. I also felt uncomfortable. I knew she loved me, but it was awkward to hear her express feelings toward this man. Still, I listened to her without anger or jealousy.

A few weeks later Sherry told this story to one of her girlfriends. Her friend listened and then told her, "Sherry, you and Brent have an intimacy that very few married couples ever have." Sherry can tell me the above story because she knows we are safe with one another. I will not retaliate in jealousy. I am not frightened anymore. We can be truthful with one another because we love each other.

However, let's imagine that Sherry were consistently unkind to me. What if she ran me down in conversations, wasted money, and made me feel unloved? Why should I be kind and loving to her if she isn't kind and loving in return? Then I think of what I learned in recovery: *There are thousands of reasons to be angry, dominating, and controlling of others. There is no justification for it.*

This statement may seem unfair. If my wife is cruel to me, why is it wrong to be unloving to her? Why can I not treat her as she treats me? If she loves me, then I will love her. If she is unkind to me, then I will pay her back. This idea is fine if I want to live in a world of revenge, but I lived in that world for eleven and a half years. I raged at my daughters because they cluttered the house and it made me miserable. I paid them back with anger. I attacked my family because I was already angry and they made me angrier.

I think of some teenagers who have a chip on their shoulder. Something happened in life that made them angry and they carry that anger within them. If I ask them to do anything that causes them more discomfort, such as mowing the lawn, cleaning up their bedroom, or washing the car, they erupt in anger. The reason is not that they are angry about what I asked them. They are already angry and my request pushes their trigger. This was how I viewed life. I was already mad when I came into the marriage, and the normal stresses of family life simply stirred up that deep-seated anger.

It does not matter what stress others bring into my life, reacting in anger does not help bring anything good. It only brings destruction to relationships. Love is the only behavior that brings healing to people. I wanted to heal and I wanted Sherry to heal. I wrote about this in my journal.

> *I believe I have lived in a 'tit for tat' mentality, not wanting to be 'used' or 'mistreated' by Sherry, afraid that I will be the only one making sacrifices in our marriage, the only one giving in. What a horrible way to be in a relationship. I reject that belief. I do not want to keep score in my marriage. I reject keeping score. I*

embrace a spirit of loving generosity toward Sherry. A spirit
that keeps no record of her wrongs, and no record of my
right behaviors.

The best example I know of love is God's love for me through his Son, Jesus Christ. Jesus died on a cross to provide forgiveness of my sins even though I did not love him. But he did it anyway. He continued to reach out in love to me to turn me from my wrongs.

Even if Sherry was as mean as the world to me (and she is quite the opposite!), I have no reason to stop loving her if I want to live a genuinely good and godly life.

The result of learning to love Sherry brought healing to her heart and reconciliation in our relationship.

The result of realizing God loved me transformed my life.

This is the miracle I live with every day.

There is one last thought I wish to communicate. I wrote this book to influence angry men to find the help I found. So their wives would be drawn to their loving husbands instead of drastically thinking how to flee. So their children would love their dads rather than being fearful of a dad who acts as an enemy. If you are an angry man, I plead with you to do the one act that no one else can do for you. *Be willing to change.*

There are **two reasons** for you to *be willing to change.*

One, because there is no bottom to what an angry person will do. My recovery leader told me that while I had never yet hit my wife, that day would come if I did not change. As hard as that was to believe, I knew that I was doing behaviors I never imagined I would do. During a fight with Sherry she left the house saying she was leaving. "Then don't come back," I screamed at her across the yard. I did not care how I failed to love my wife. I let anger speak for me. I spanked my daughters so hard, not to discipline them, but to punish them with my rage. I verbally assaulted their self-image, causing them to feel there was something wrong with them. I did not care if I hurt them. To this day they are dealing with the emotional trauma of an abusive dad. Therefore, if I continued on my destructive path, eventually what else would I do?

I see the downward spiral in so many destructive behaviors. An alcoholic never thinks that someday they might be living under a bridge begging for money when they currently live in a beautiful home and have a wonderful job. A successful actor doesn't think their drug habit will eventually kill them, but we read such accounts on a regular basis. Someone with an addiction to pornography, that started as a teenager, never thinks they would be interested in children, but eventually they are arrested for trafficking in child pornography. None of these people thought they would descend so low in their behaviors, but they did because of the choices they made long ago.

When I was twelve years old, I sensed God warning me about my temper. I never considered that forty-three years later my wife and daughters would leave me because of my anger. But that is what happened because I failed to deal with the warnings I received.

As a teenager I spent a number of wonderful summer days at a riverside park. My friends and I would stand on a bridge thirty-five feet above the water as we stepped over the guard, fearfully hanging on the railing, waiting for the courage to launch into the air. When we let go, there was a three-second freefall as your stomach came up in your throat until we thundered into the river. There were salamanders to catch and upstream were boulders to climb and places to explore.

At the bottom of the rapids the water poured off a waterfall into a pool. Next to the river was a large boulder. We plunged into the tumultuous pool of swirling water. You could not see anything because of all the air bubbles. Everything was white. The current from the rapids twisted and swirled your body as you fought to remain upright. We were a hundred feet downstream when we came up for air. It was like jumping into a giant collection of air bubbles suspended underwater.

My friend Tim decided to look at a pool of water to the side of the boulder from which we jumped. I heard a splash. I looked down and saw that Tim had slipped off the rocks into the water. I started to laugh at his fall. He went under water. Eventually he surfaced. Only the circle of his face rose to the air. He looked troubled.

"Help," he cried, faintly.

Under the water he disappeared as the whirlpool sucked him down again.

He rose one last time. Then he went back under. There was a huge splash. Steve, his older brother, flew off the rock and into the water beside him. I do not know if Steve pushed him out of the whirlpool with his hands, or if the force of his body thundering into the water drove Tim out, but they both disappeared from the torrent.

Moments went by with no sight of them. A hundred feet downstream Tim surfaced and weakly swam to the shore. No sight of Steve. Finally, he appeared and lay beside his brother on the beach. Exhausted but alive.

Anger is like a jumping into a raging river. I did not know that hidden very near were whirlpools that would suck me down into behaviors I never thought I would practice. It killed the very life of my family, my marriage, and my soul. I was being pulled down a path of destruction to Sherry, Ellie, Nikki, and me. I was drowning in the tumbled mess of broken family relationships.

The truth of the matter is there is no bottom to how bad it will get. This is one whirlpool that just goes deeper and deeper over time.

So what is the other reason for you to *be willing to change?*

Two, "If you do not change, then others will change you." I saw this in my life when Sherry and the girls left. I see it when the police arrest a drunk driver. I see it when a judge sentences a sex offender to prison, or orders a domestic abuser to attend a recovery program. The truth is, if we do not obey the warnings of our conscience and change our thinking and behavior, then others will step in to change us. I so wish I would have followed the warnings I received early in my life so that I could have raised my daughters, and been a husband to my wife, without anger and domination. Unfortunately, I failed to do so.

It is my hope that this book will influence you to seek the help you need for anger. If you don't, someday someone else will do it for you. My experience has been that when someone else tries to make us willing to change, it always is much more painful than if we changed ourselves.

It is my hope that you are willing and ready to change.

I wish you the very best!

Acknowledgments

Many people helped bring me out of the darkness and into the light. Sherry did not know if I would become physically violent, steal our money, divorce her, or enter into a custody fight when she left. But she took the risk to save our daughters and herself from my abuse. I am so grateful that she helped herself, our daughters, and eventually me.

Sherry's sister and brother-in-law, Connie and Joe Matis, housed and supported Sherry, Ellie, and Nikki during the year they lived with them. I am deeply grateful to them for the help they gave my family.

Abuse Recovery Ministries and Services (ARMS) is the recovery program I joined. The founder and director, Stacy Womack, helped save my life, helped Sherry in her recovery, and our marriage. Her leadership, along with her husband, Jerry Womack, and numerous facilitators, transformed me. I do not believe anyone can recover from abuse unless they have the help of others to change the way they think. An anger management program will, in my opinion, not change the deep-seated lies in a man that cause him to abuse his family. ARMS does not help manage anger. Instead, it works to transform the way men think. If you know you need help, please call them at 503-846-9284. They also provide outstanding counseling to women who have been abused by angry men.

Ken Nair's book, *Discovering the Mind of a Woman: The Key to Becoming a Strong and Irresistible Husband*, was the primary textbook we used in my recovery program. This author gave me hope that if I transformed, I would eventually reconcile with my wife and become the husband she desired.

The people of Won By One church, pastored by Jack Shumate, along with his wife, Shelly, helped Sherry. While not condoning my behavior, they did not condemn me. Instead they prayed for me to change and for our family to be saved. Tim and Nancy Burton housed me when Sherry, Ellie, and Nikki returned home. I am so grateful to this congregation.

My in-laws loved me throughout all the years of my sin, and continued to love me during the separation. My mother-in-law, Ruby Kurtz, forgave me even though I had terribly hurt her daughter and granddaughters. Sherry's sister and brother-in-law, Linda and Kurt Otness, supported Sherry, did not reject me, and totally embraced my efforts to change. They loved me in spite of the hurt I caused them.

I broke the heart of my parents, Emmett and Reta Hofer, but they continued to pray that reconciliation would happen without throwing shame and guilt on me. My dad lived long enough to see Sherry and me reconcile, for which I am so grateful.

Heart Change, at House of Myrrh Ministries, is the name of the workshop I attended to overcome fear and discover God's love for me. Seven years later I still use the tools they taught me. People come from all over the country to attend. They can be reached at 503-557-5050.

My personal counselor, Elliot Klearman, helped me see that anxiety did not have to be the hallmark of my life. I am so grateful for the hope he gave me. I encourage anyone dealing with anger to see a personal counselor and discover the root of why they are angry.

Four friends did not leave me during the separation. They loved Sherry and me and they walked with us. Alan and Lori Bailey, and Steve and Leta Fortier, gave of themselves to us. They continue to be dear friends of ours.

Meagan Kowaleski is the young woman who warned Sherry that she was being abused by me and needed help. If not for her support, Sherry would have never joined a domestic abuse class, let alone taken the steps to open my eyes. Thank you, Meagan! You started the process of healing.

Devota Robins helped Sherry immensely in preparation for separating from me, including moving, finances, and emotional support.

My daughters, Ellie (Eleanna) and Nikki (Nicole) lived through horrible years. I do not deserve to be their dad, let alone Sherry's husband. Thank you for giving me another chance to live right with each of you!

David Sanford is my outstanding editor. Thank you, Kelly Bard, for telling him about my book idea. David emailed and asked to meet with me, saying that he had prayed for a book like this to be published. He encouraged me to write this confessional and taught me a number of new writing skills. Thank you, David. Thanks too to Rachel Mortimer for proofreading this book before it went to press.

There are countless others who assisted Sherry and our daughters, people I am unaware of, who helped my family survive. Thank you so much for loving my family.

Finally, none of this would have happened if God did not love me and my family. God used all these people and so many more to save my family and me. Thank you, Lord!

Made in the USA
Columbia, SC
17 March 2019